Drayton Bird

∞0

21 August 2016

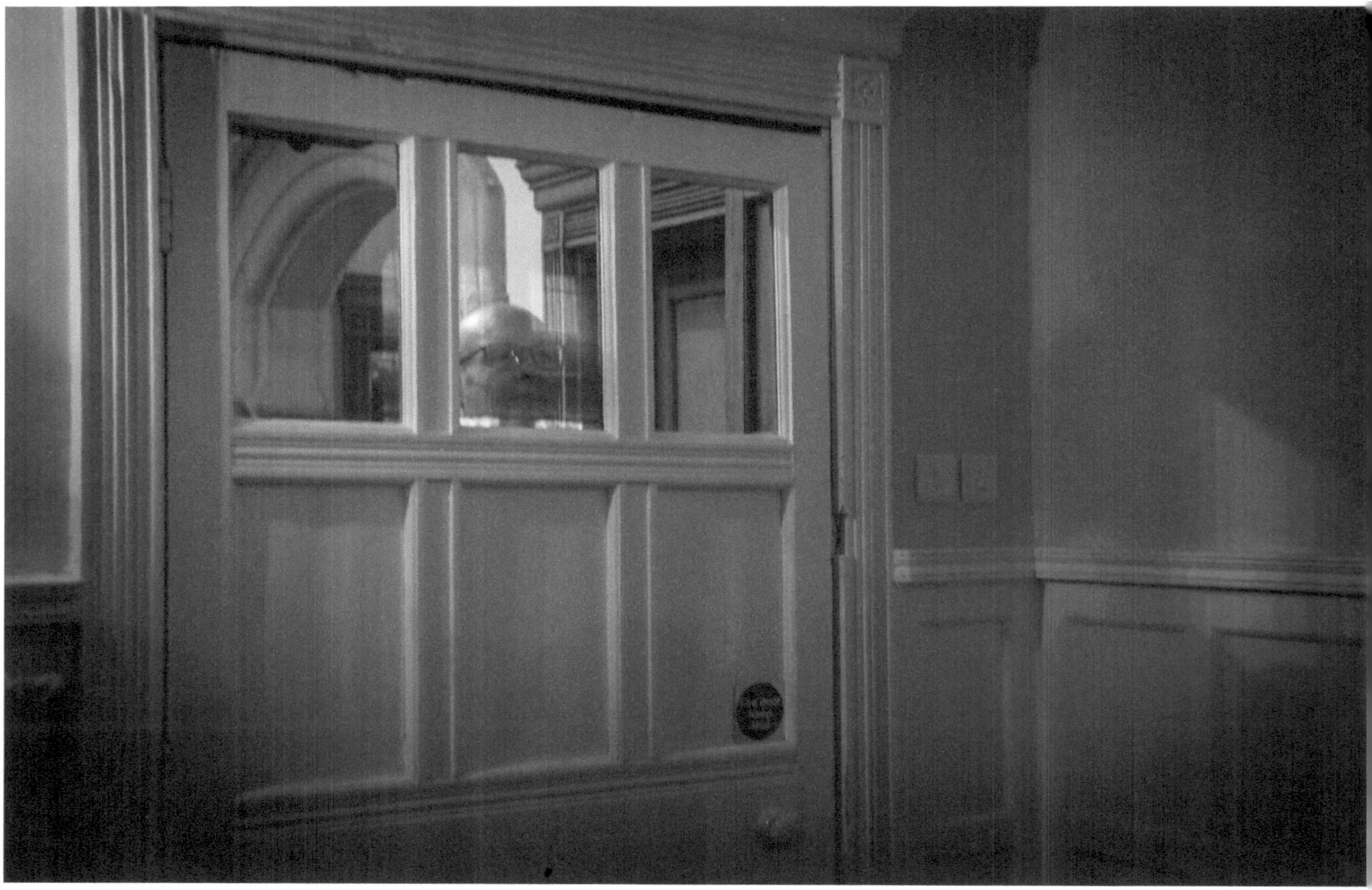

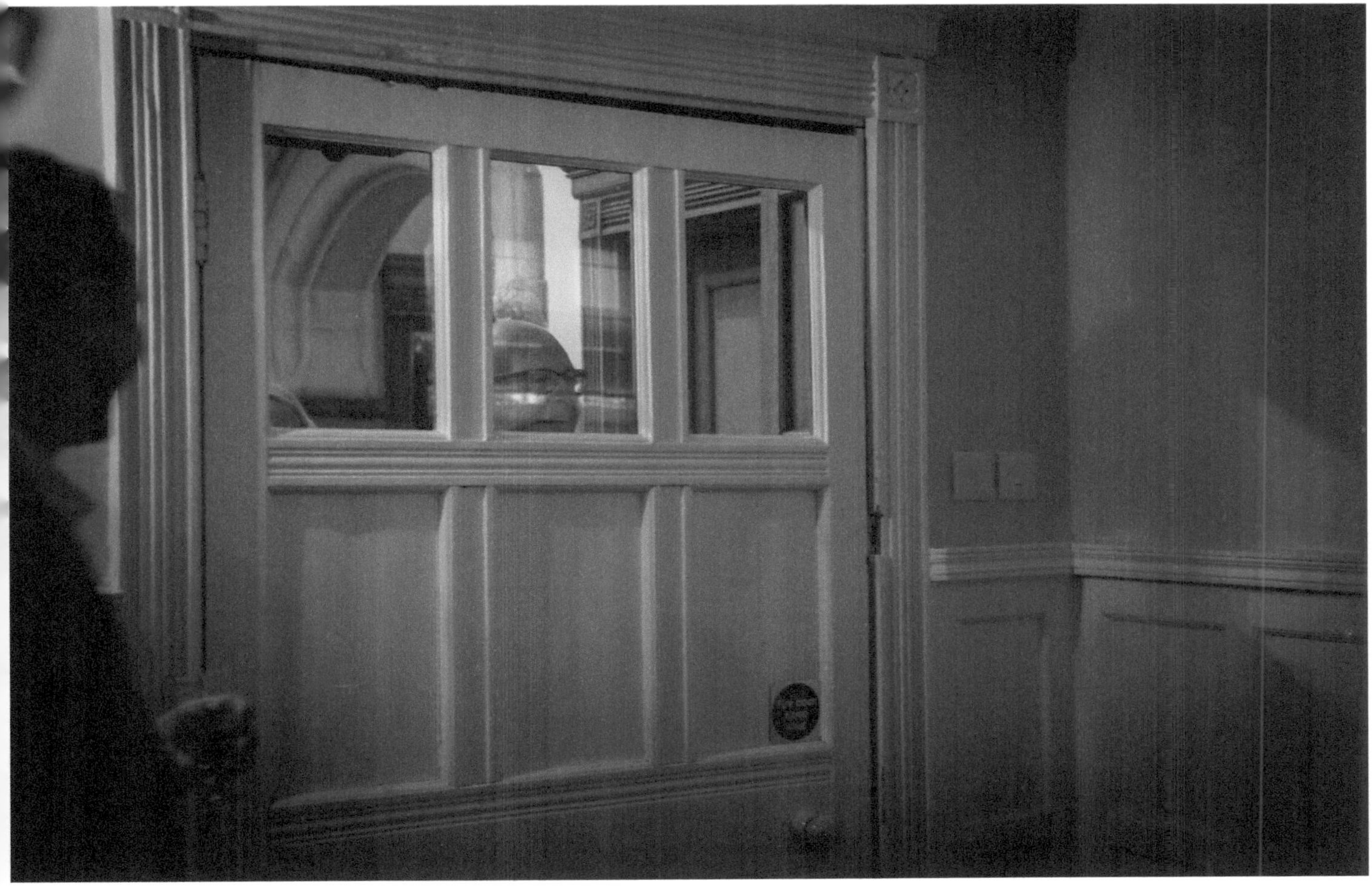

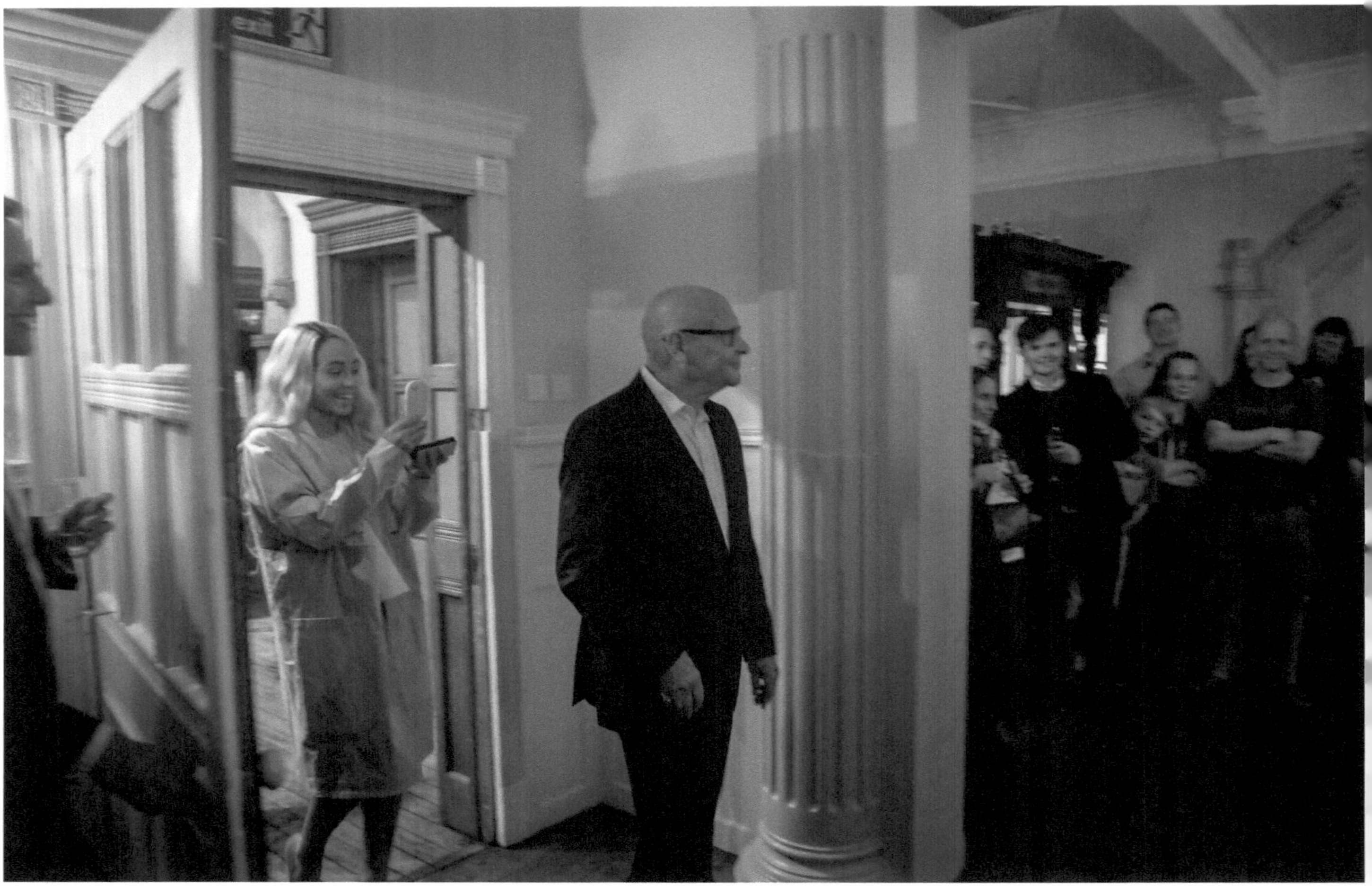

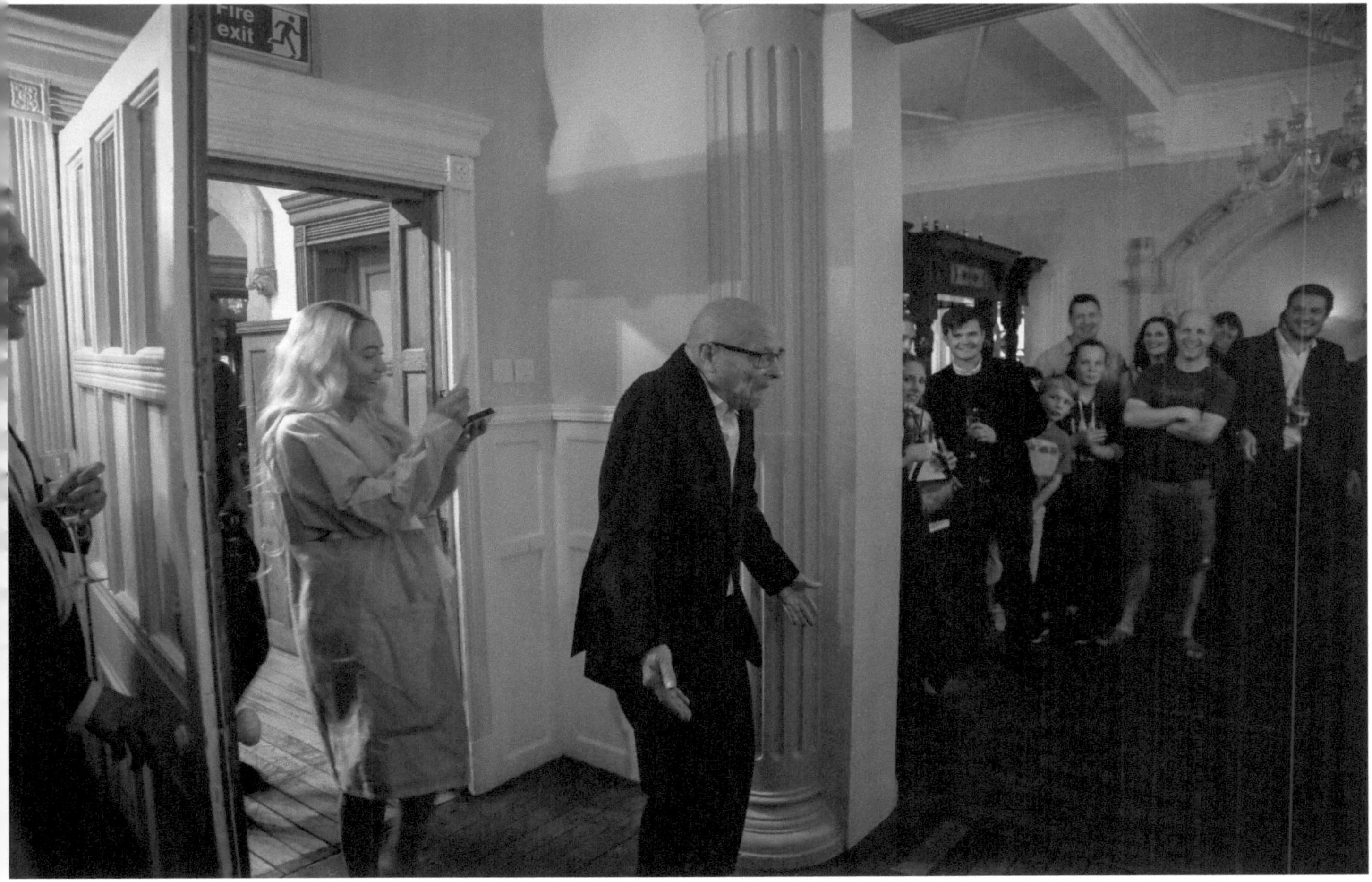
Fire
exit

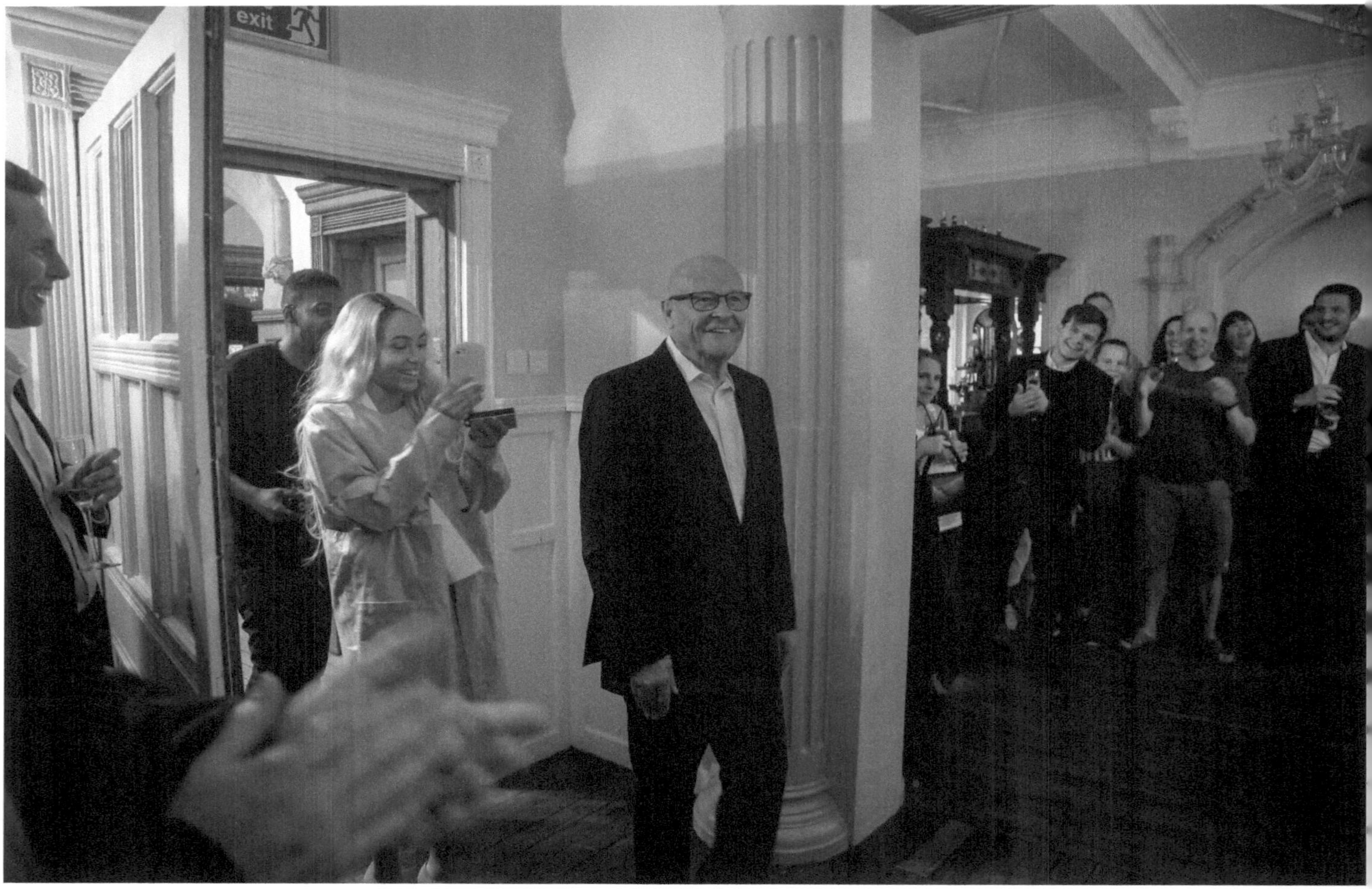
exit

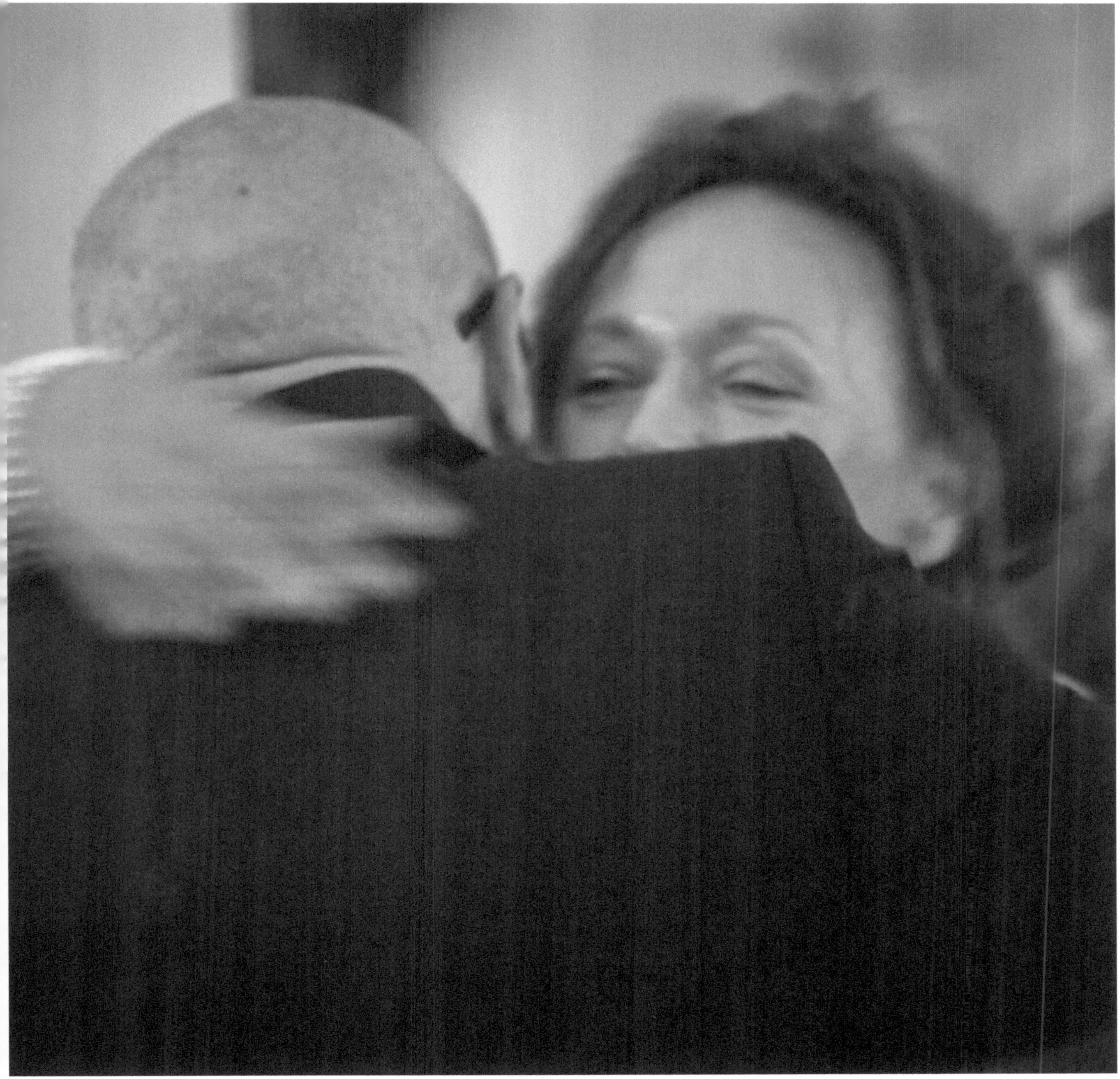

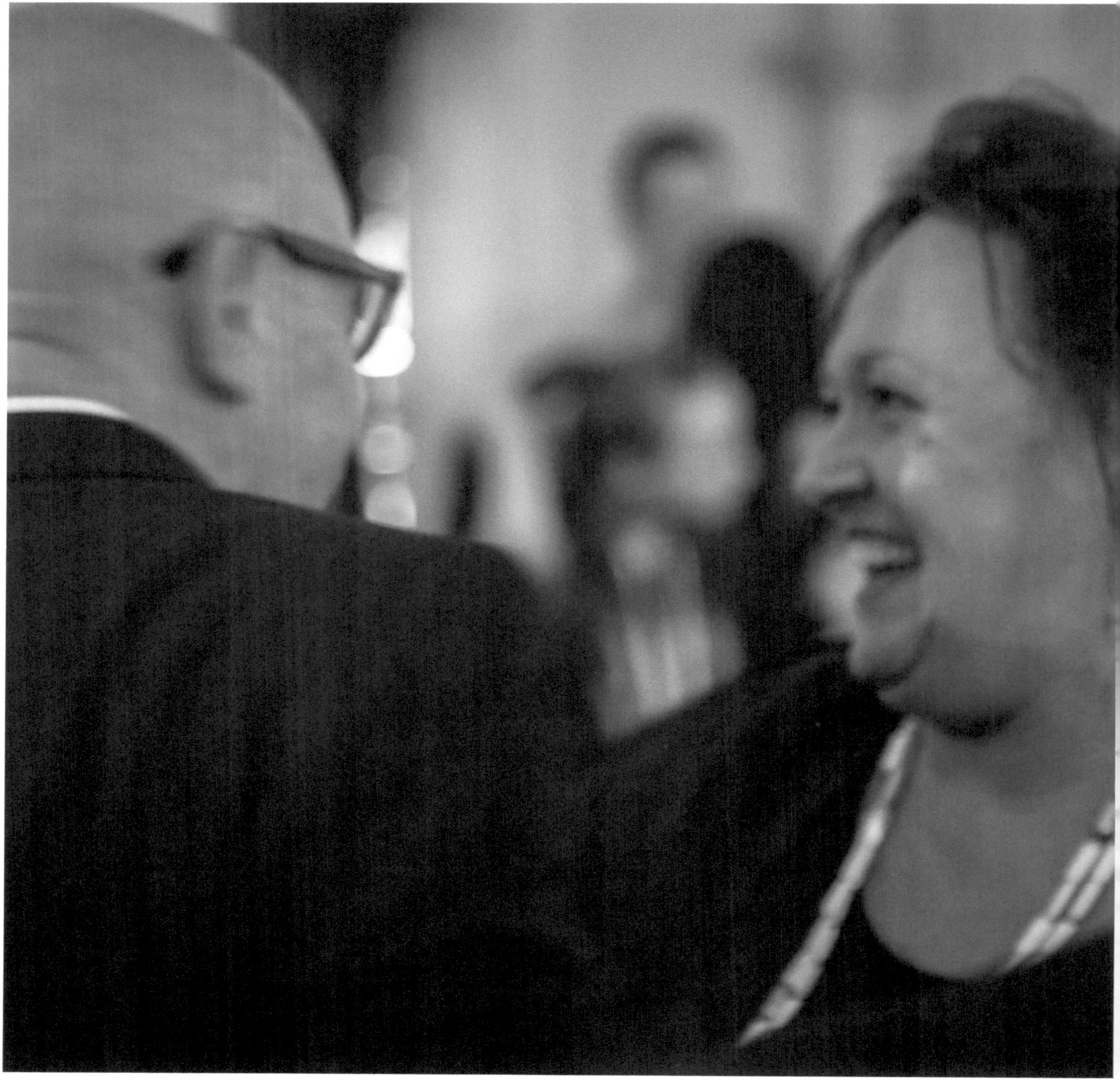

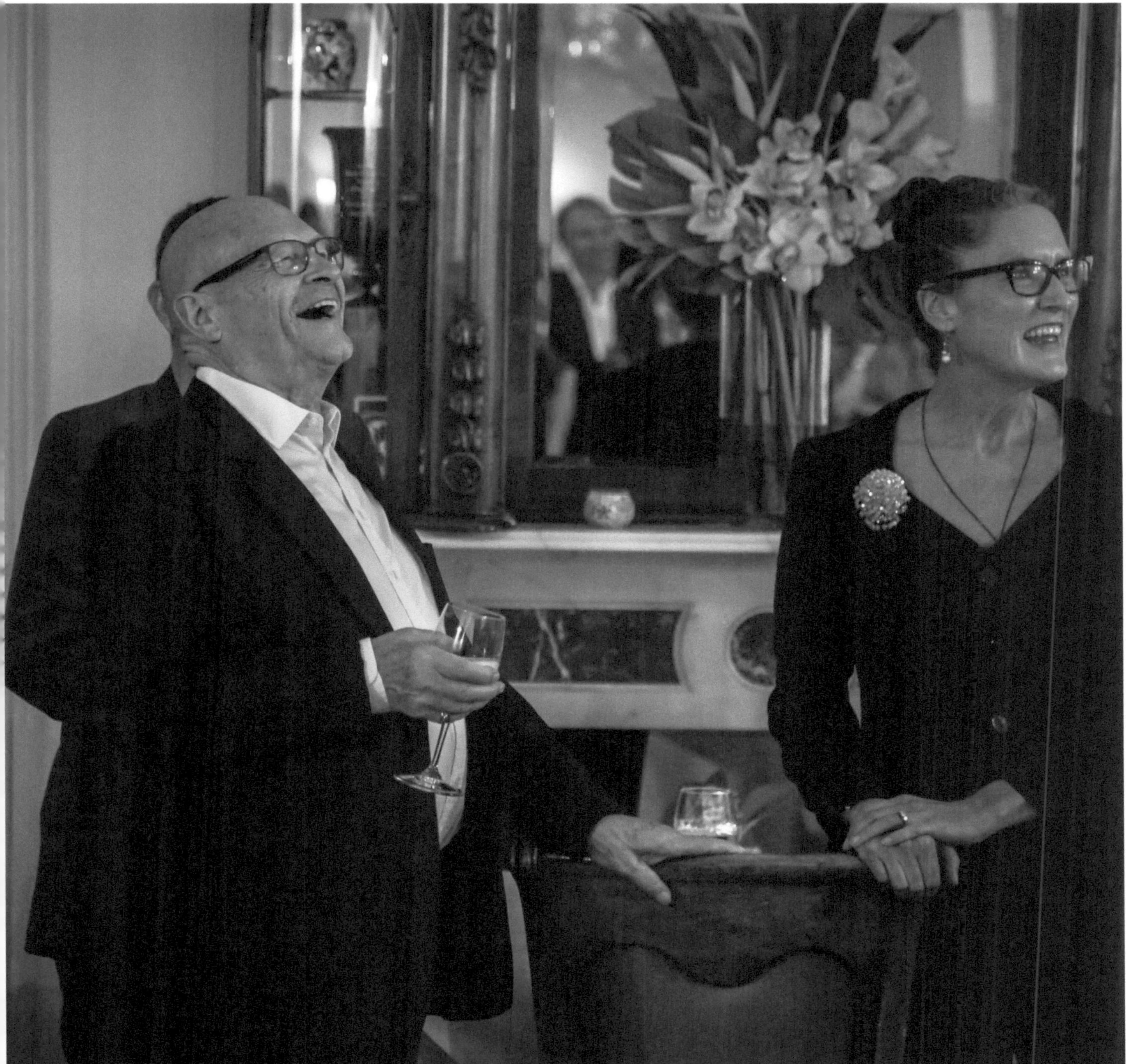

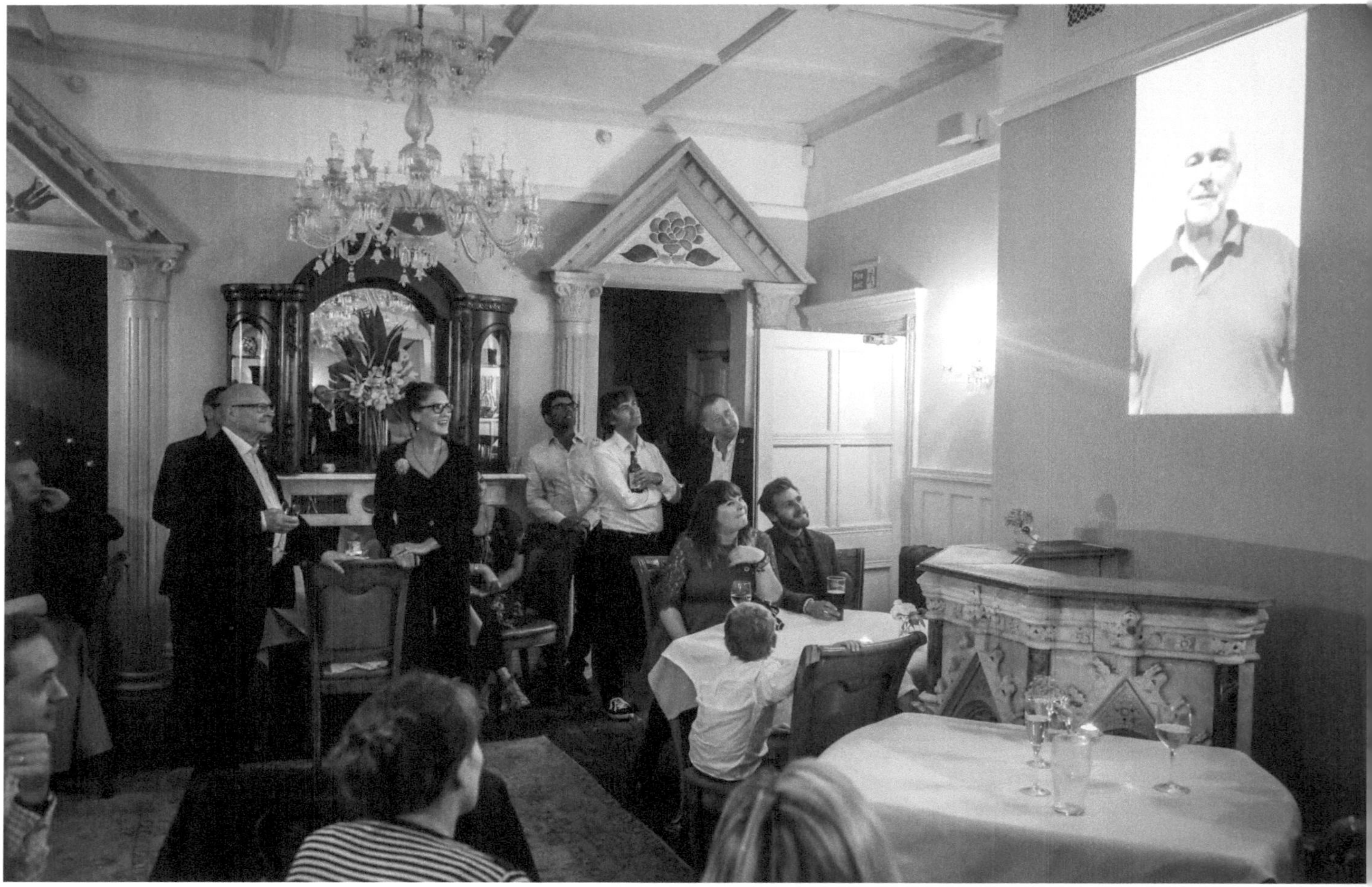

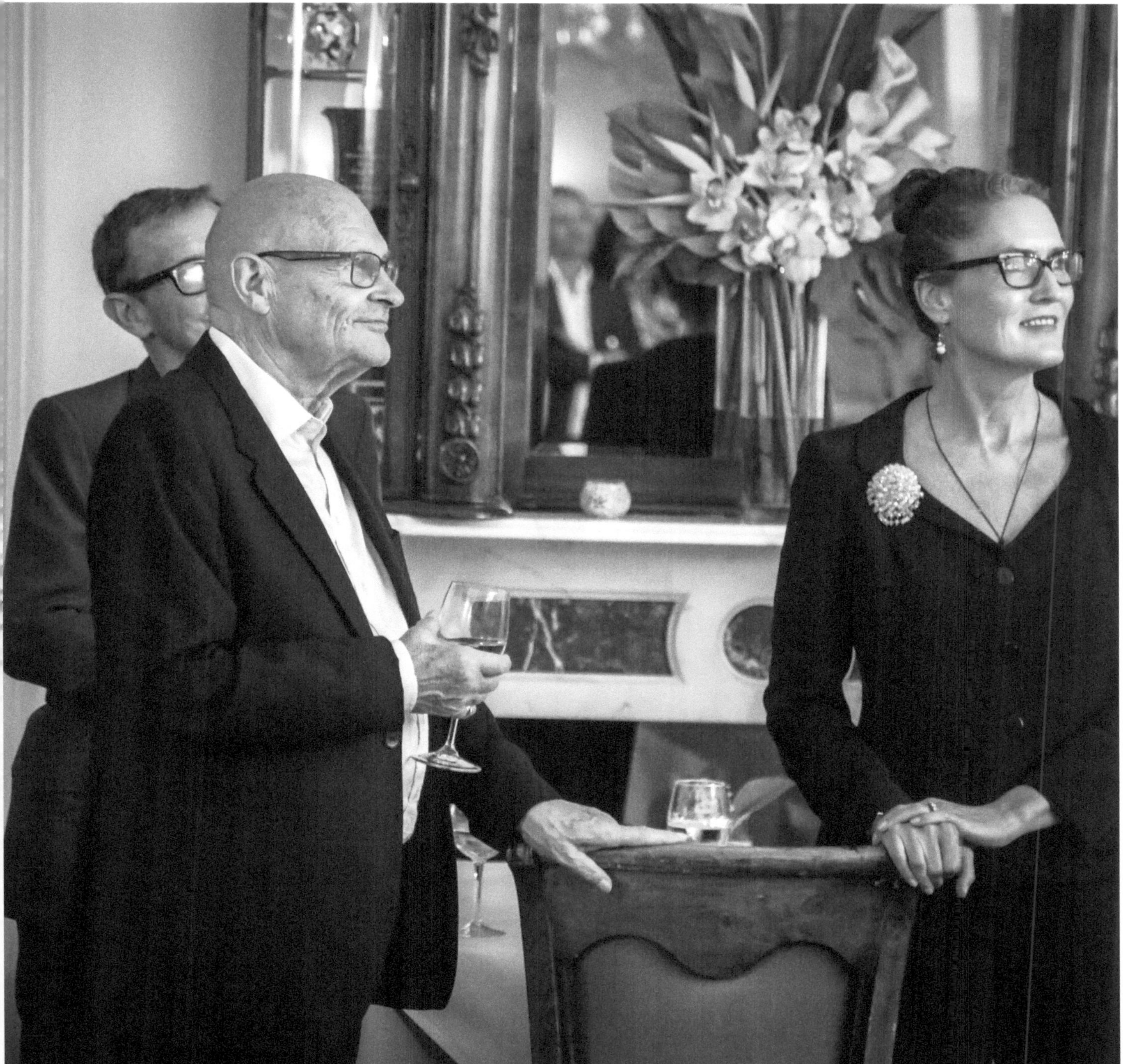

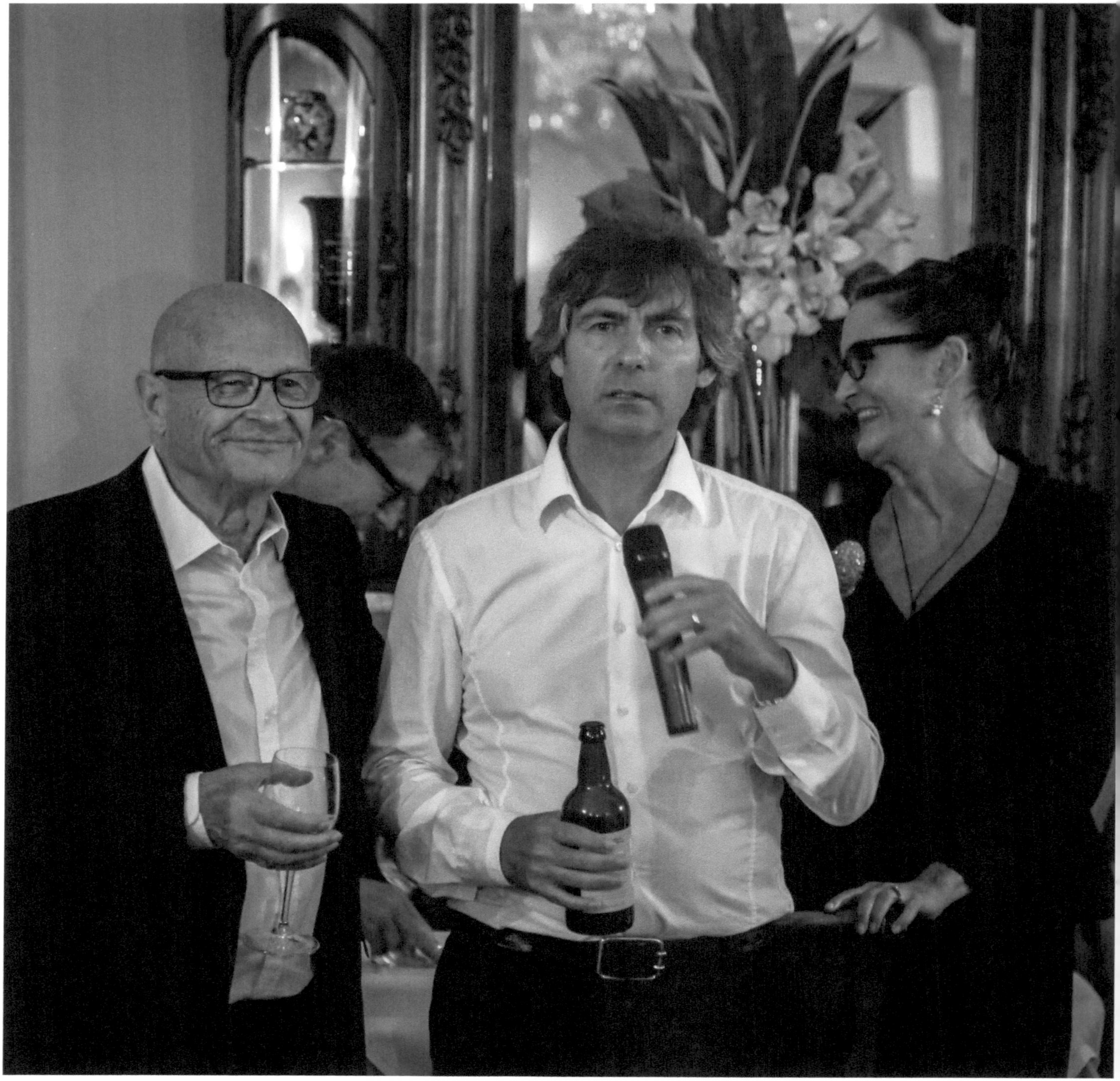

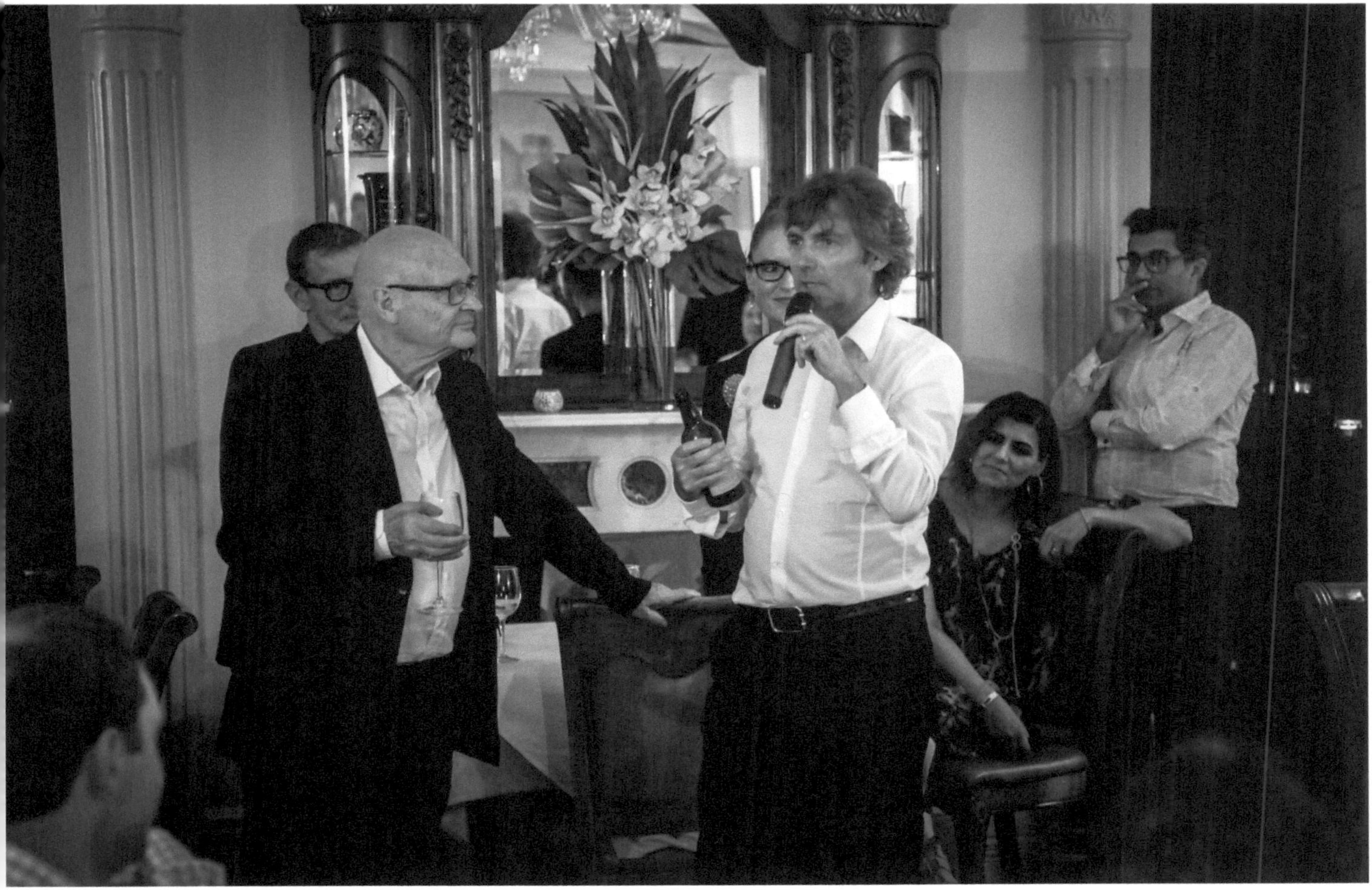

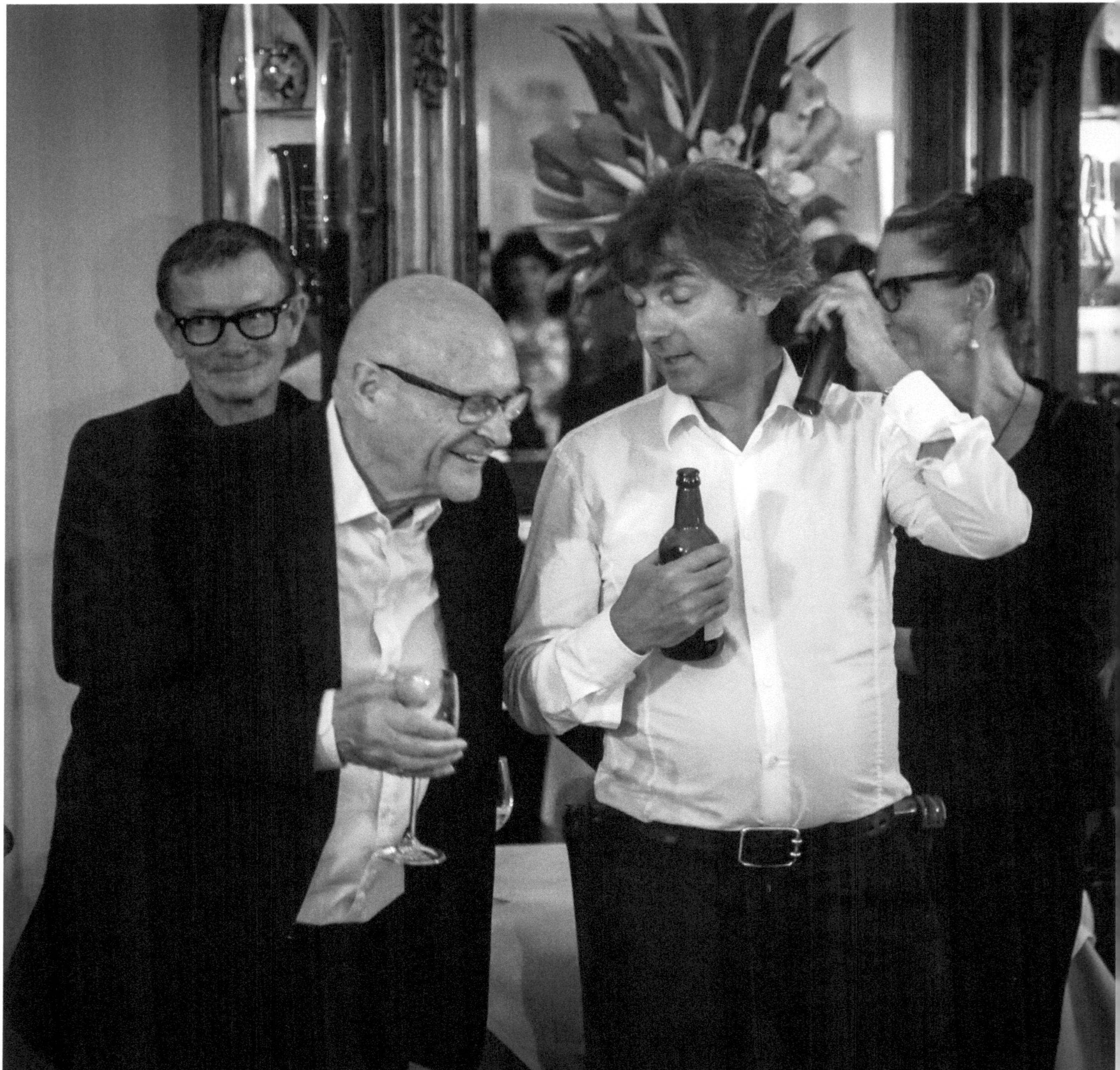

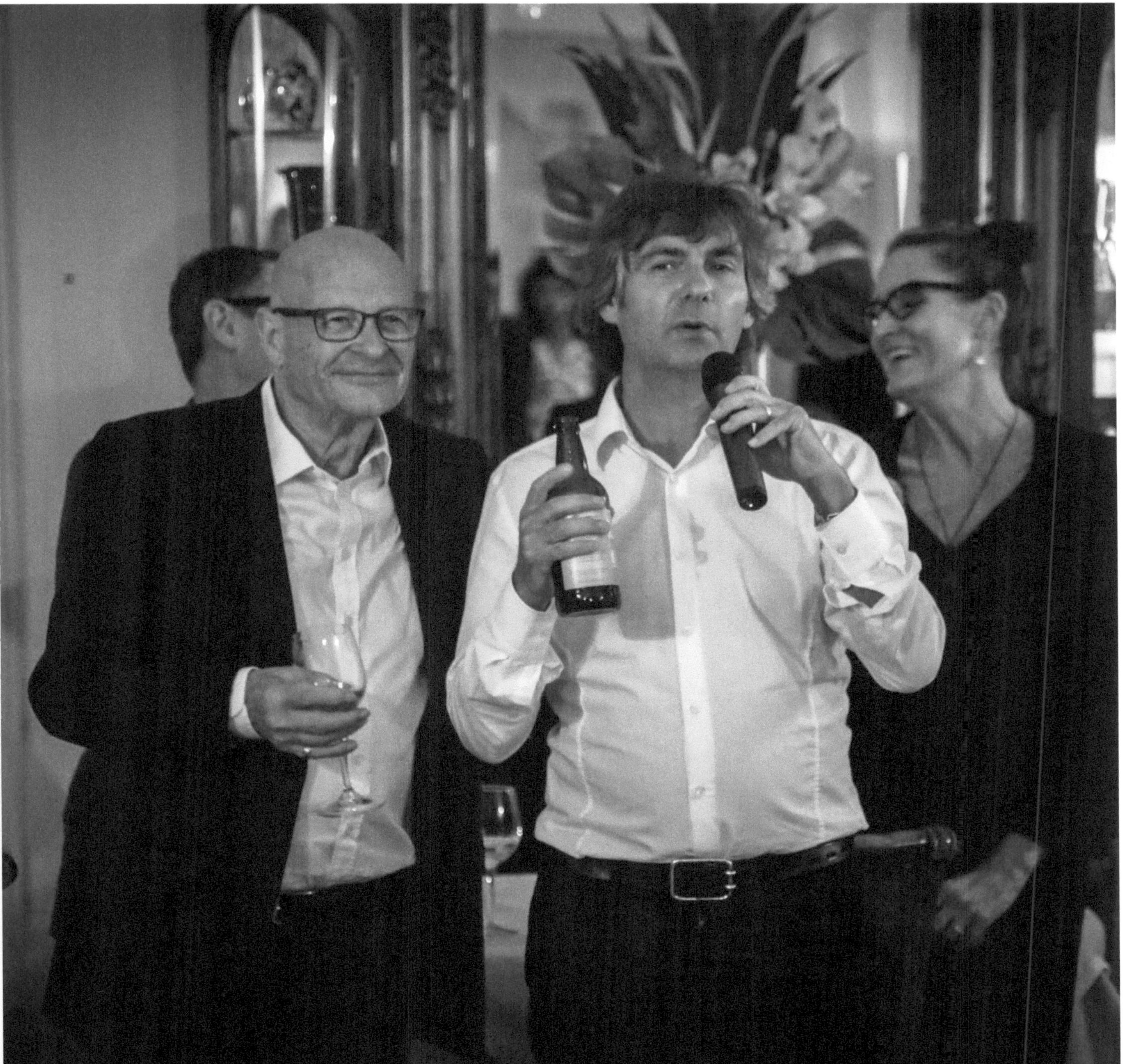

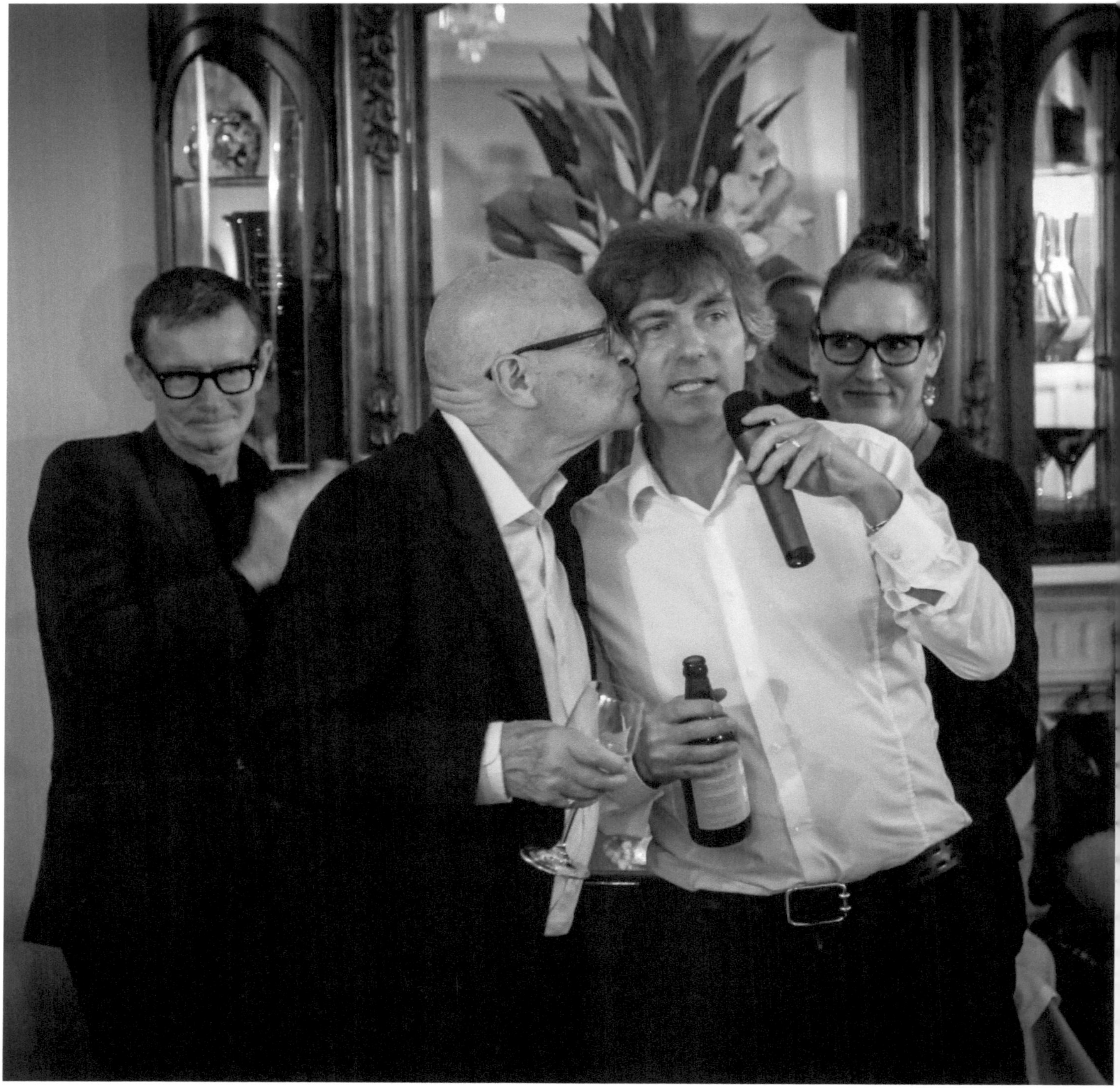

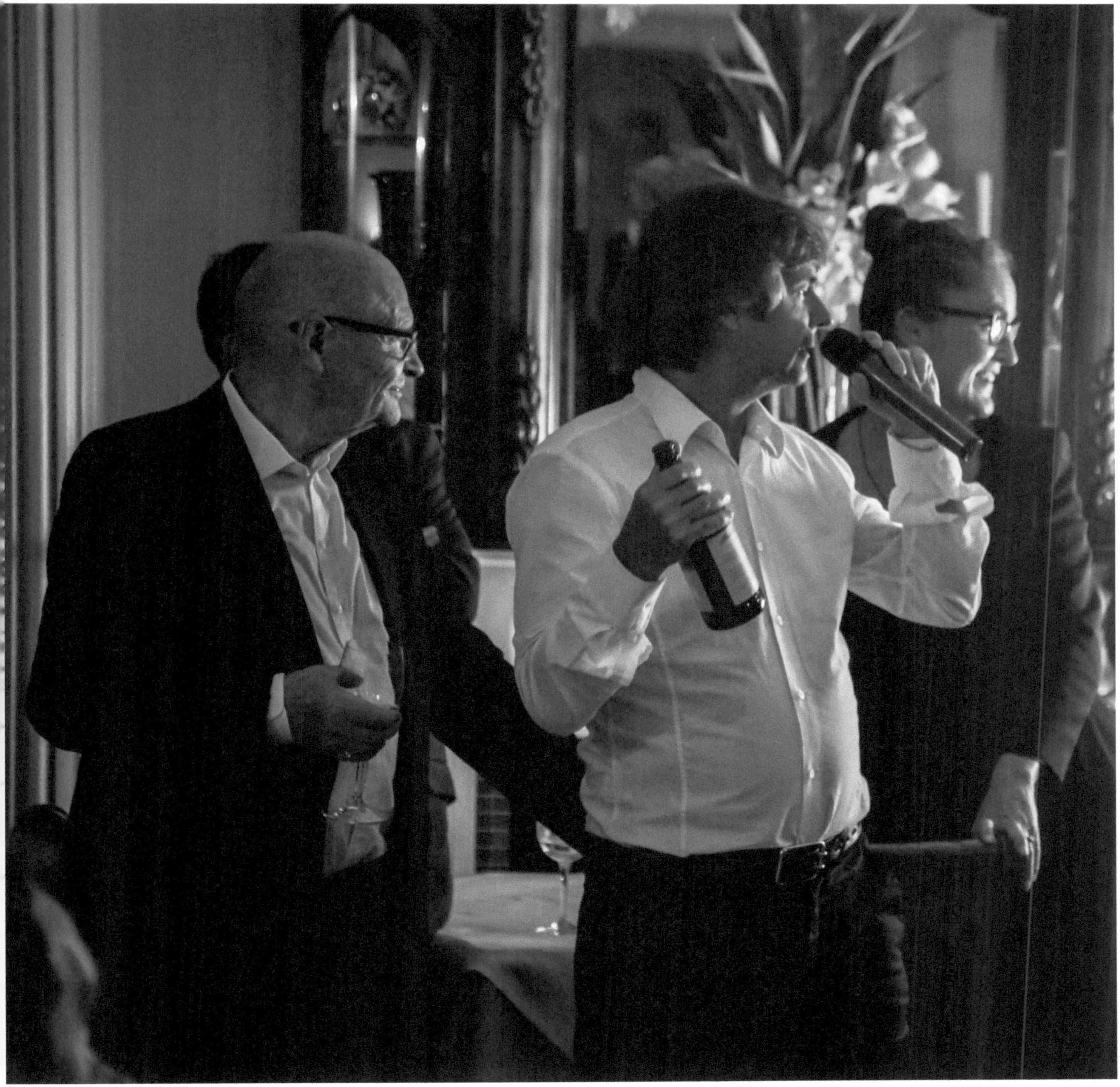

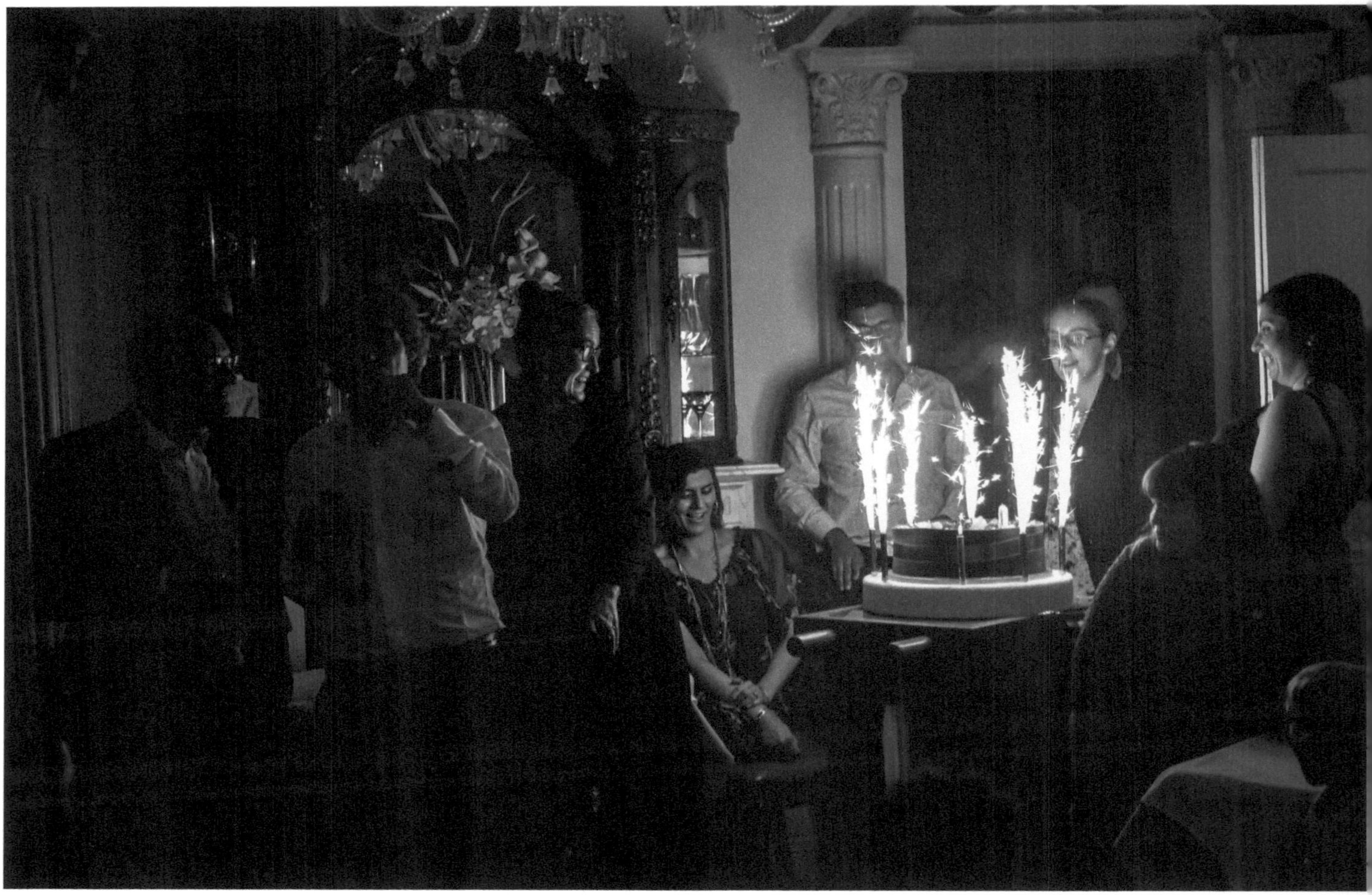

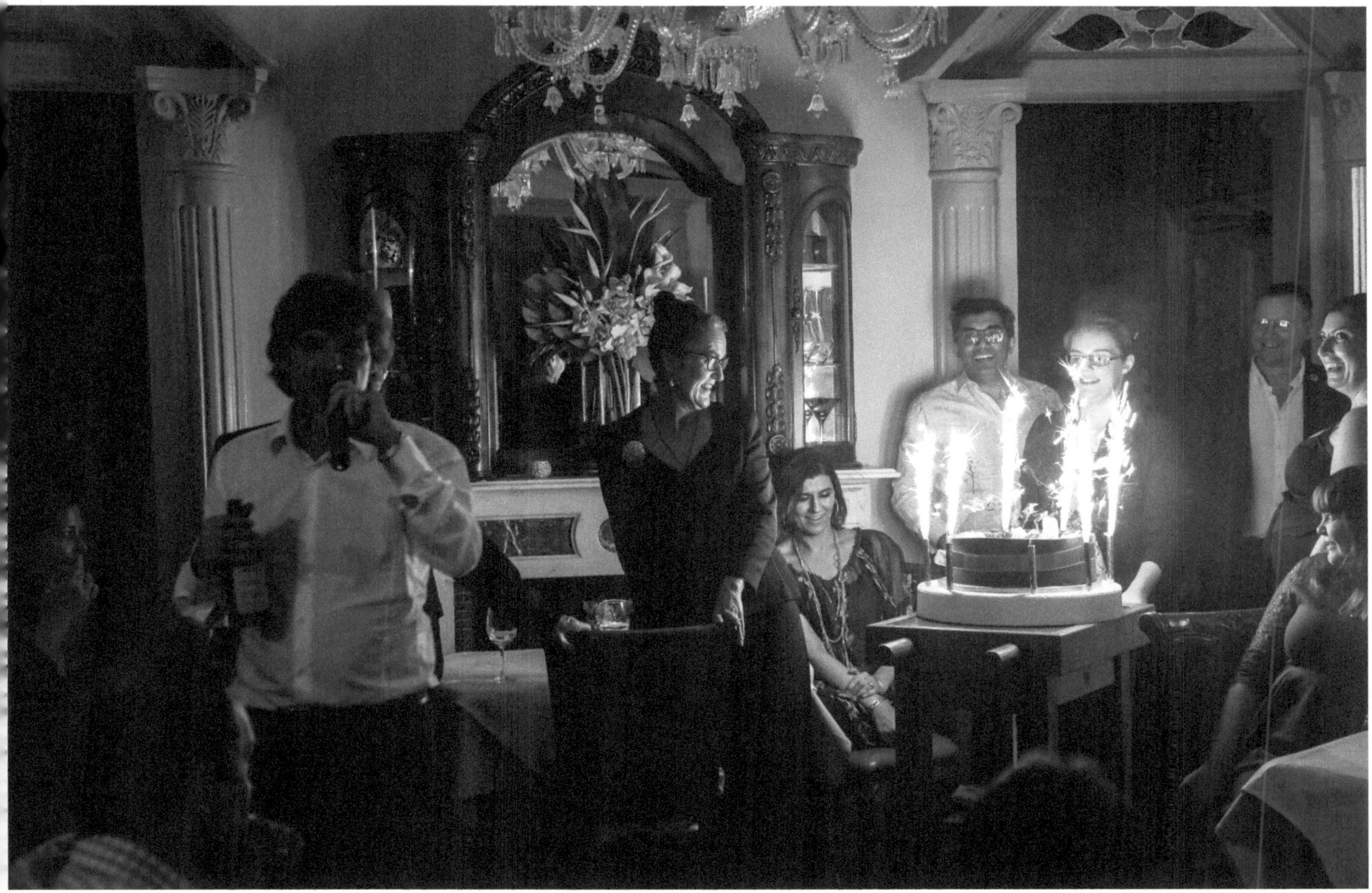

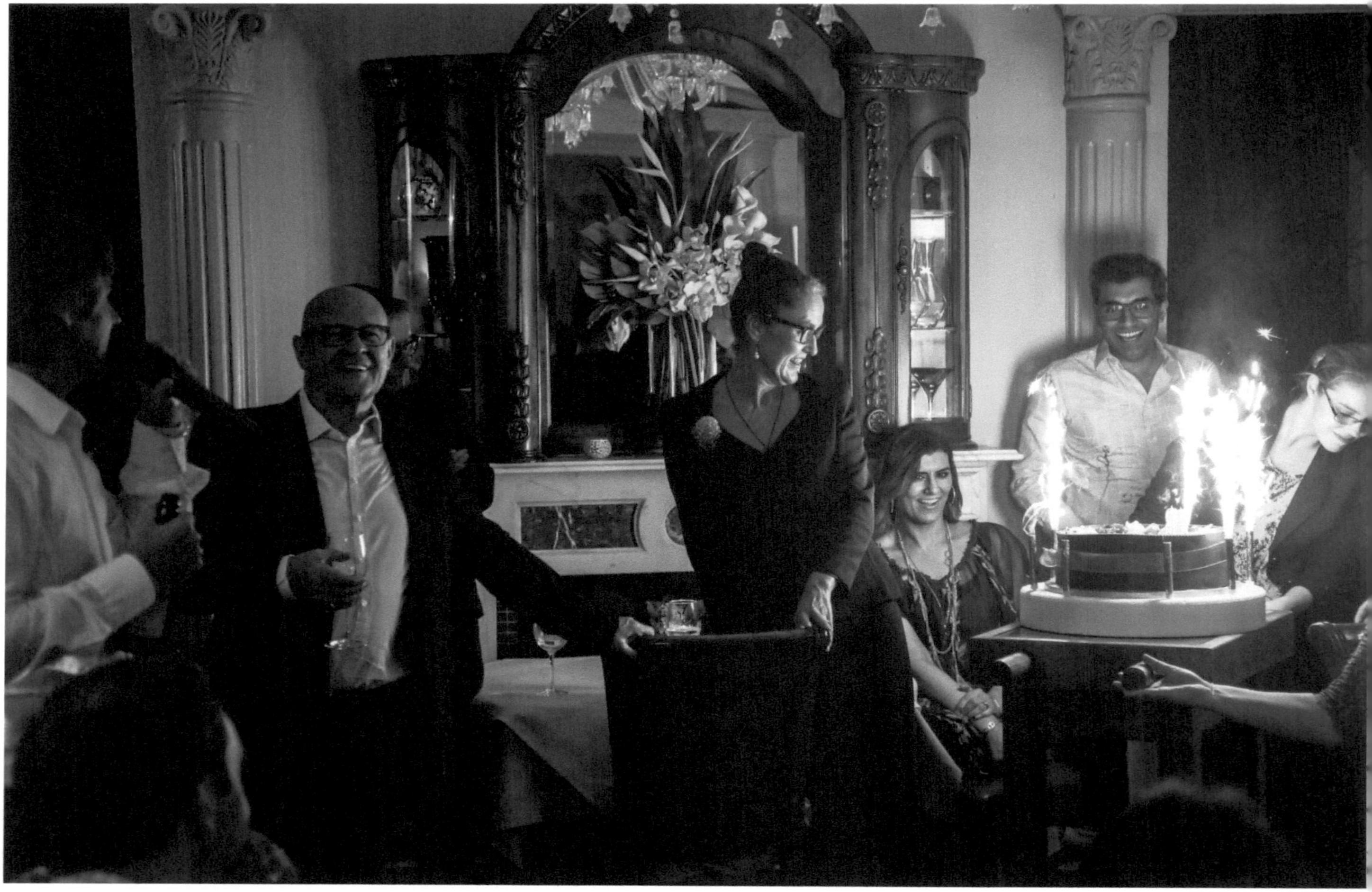

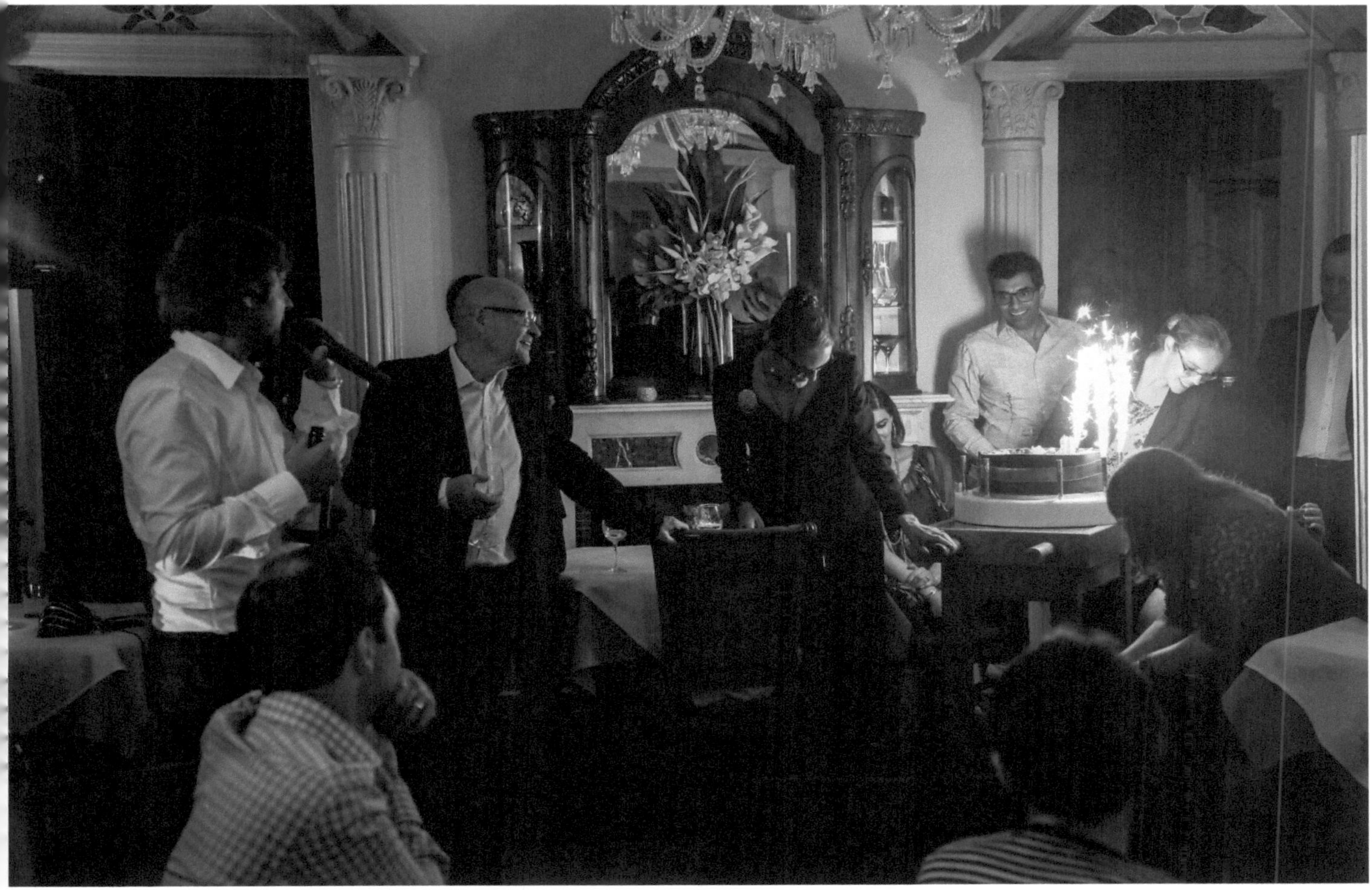

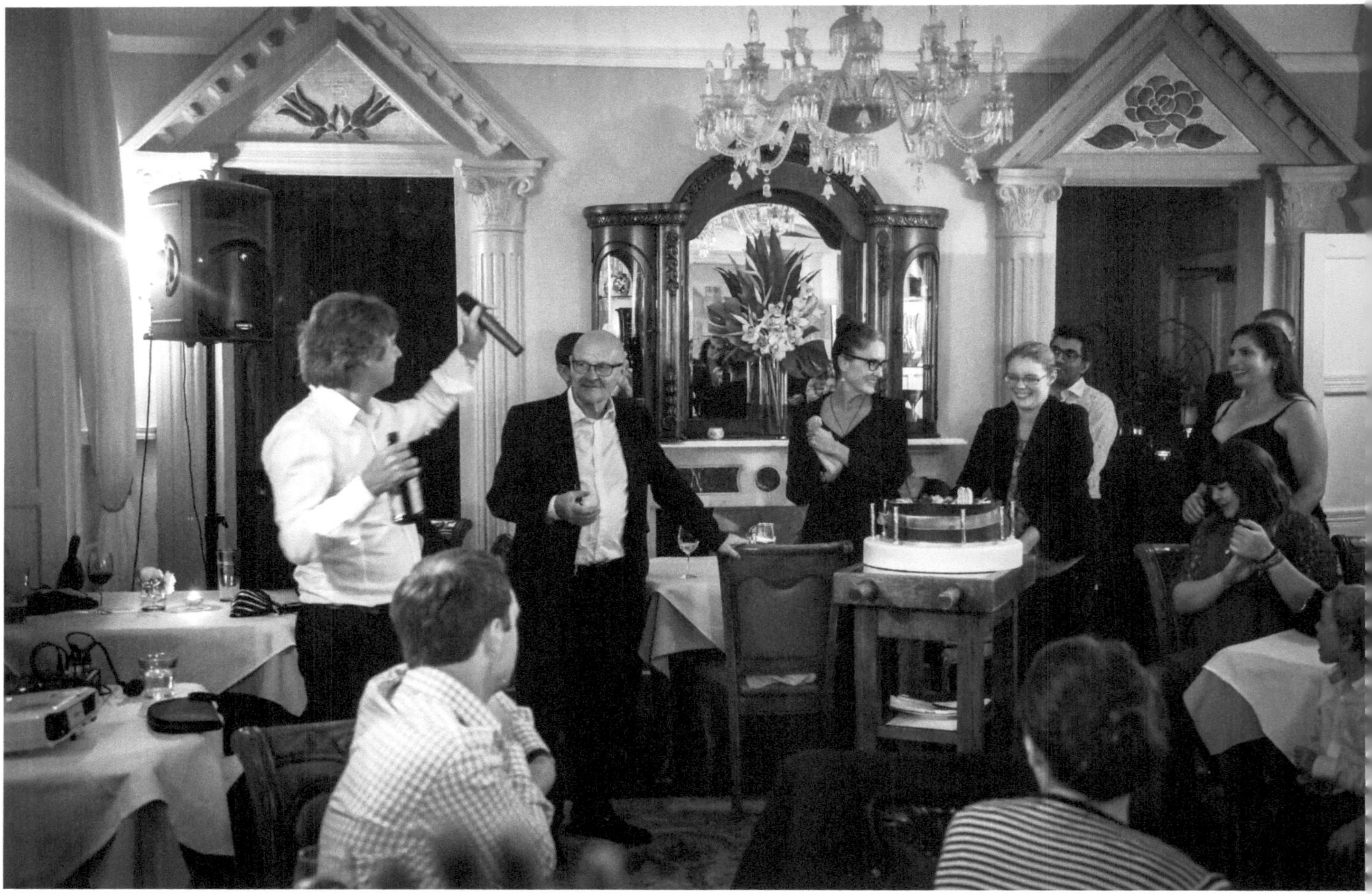

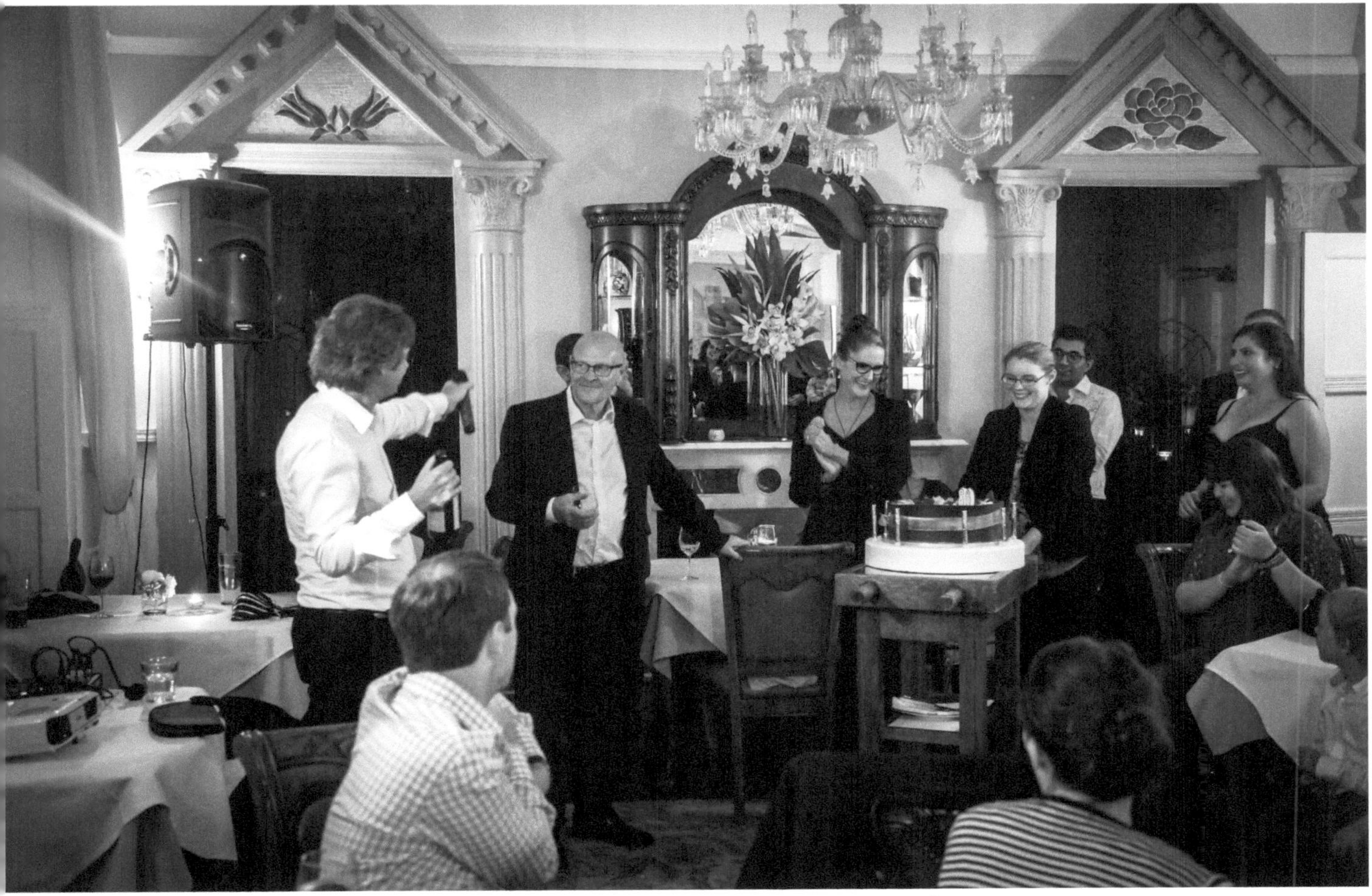

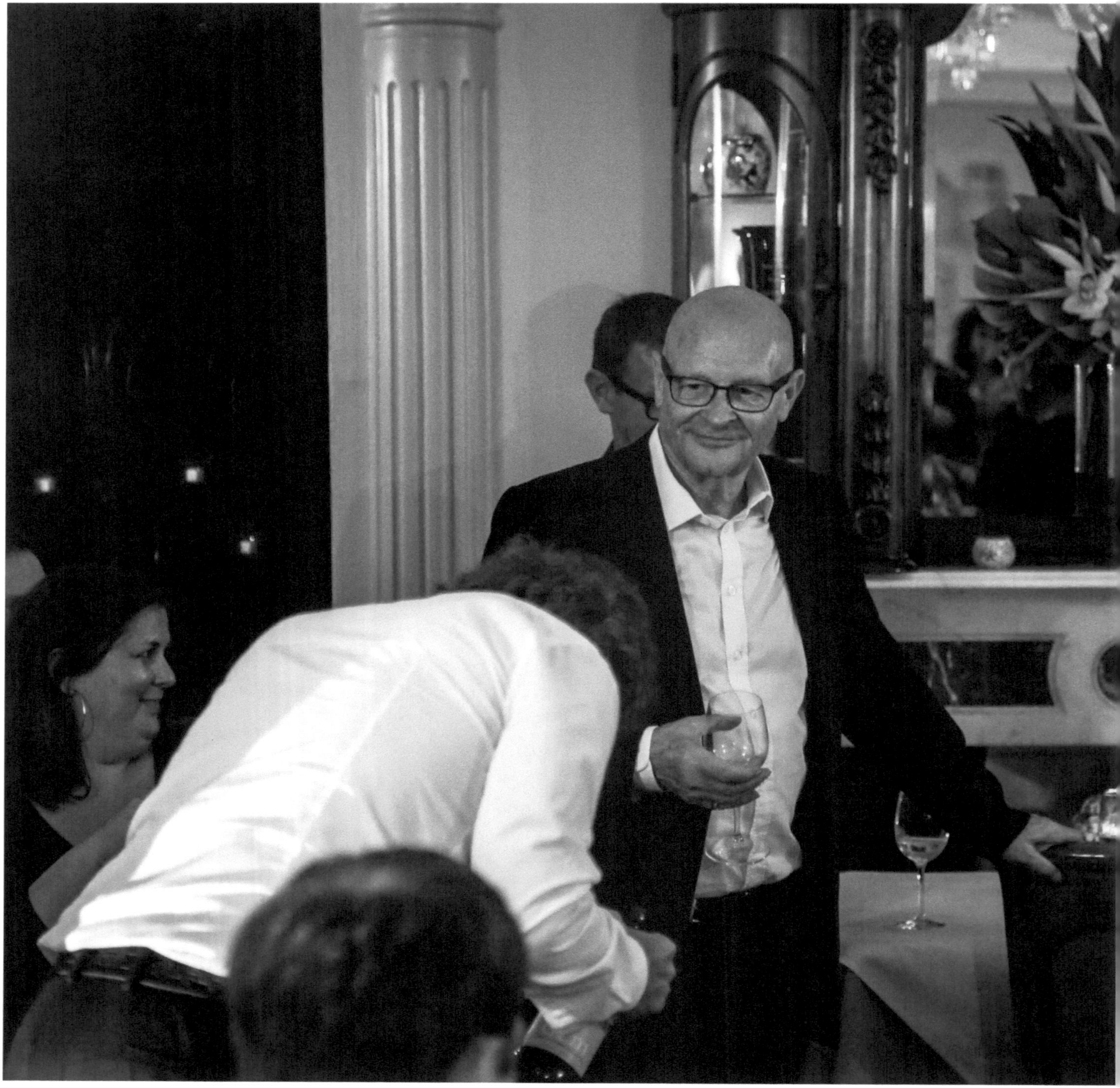

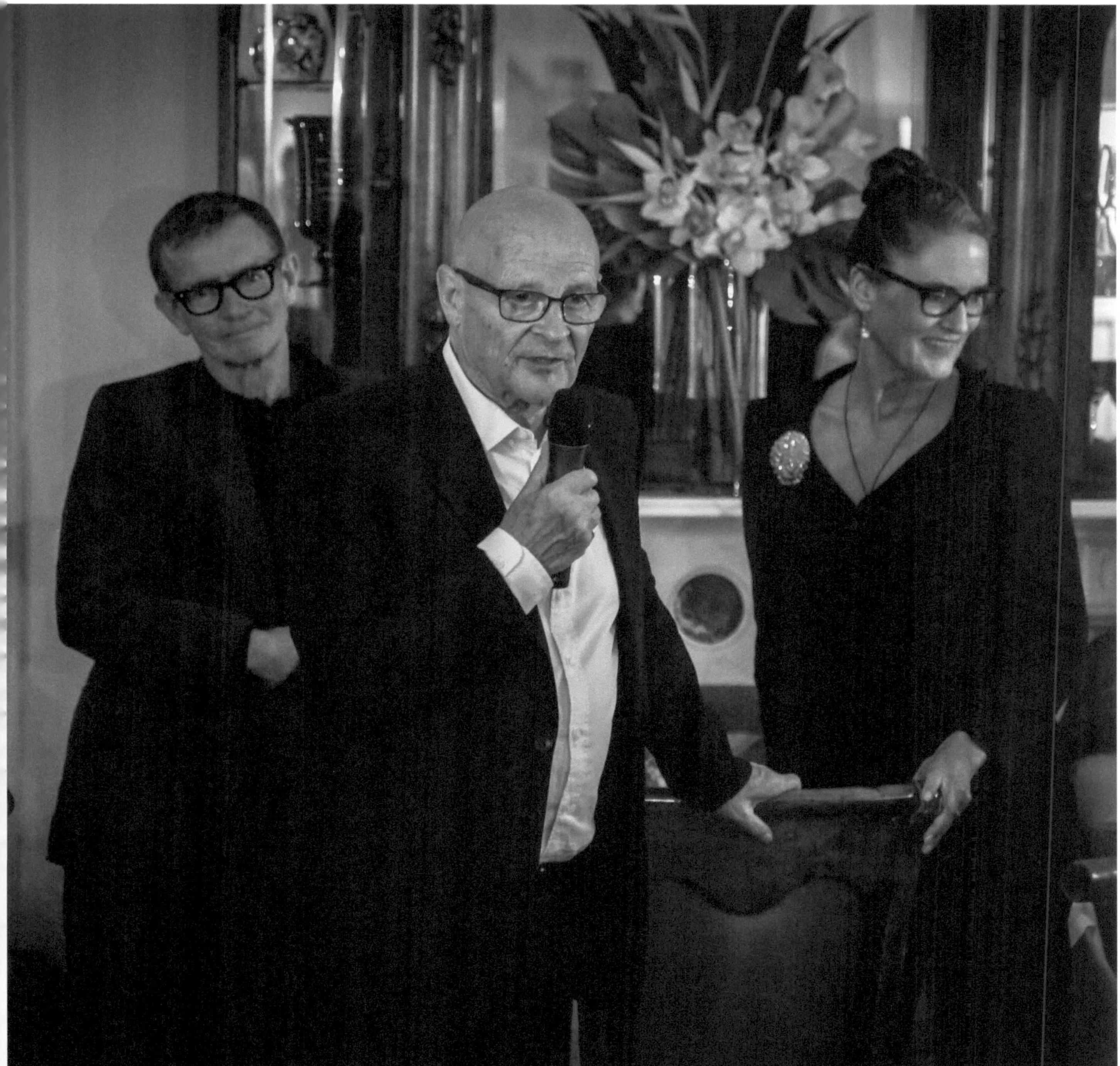

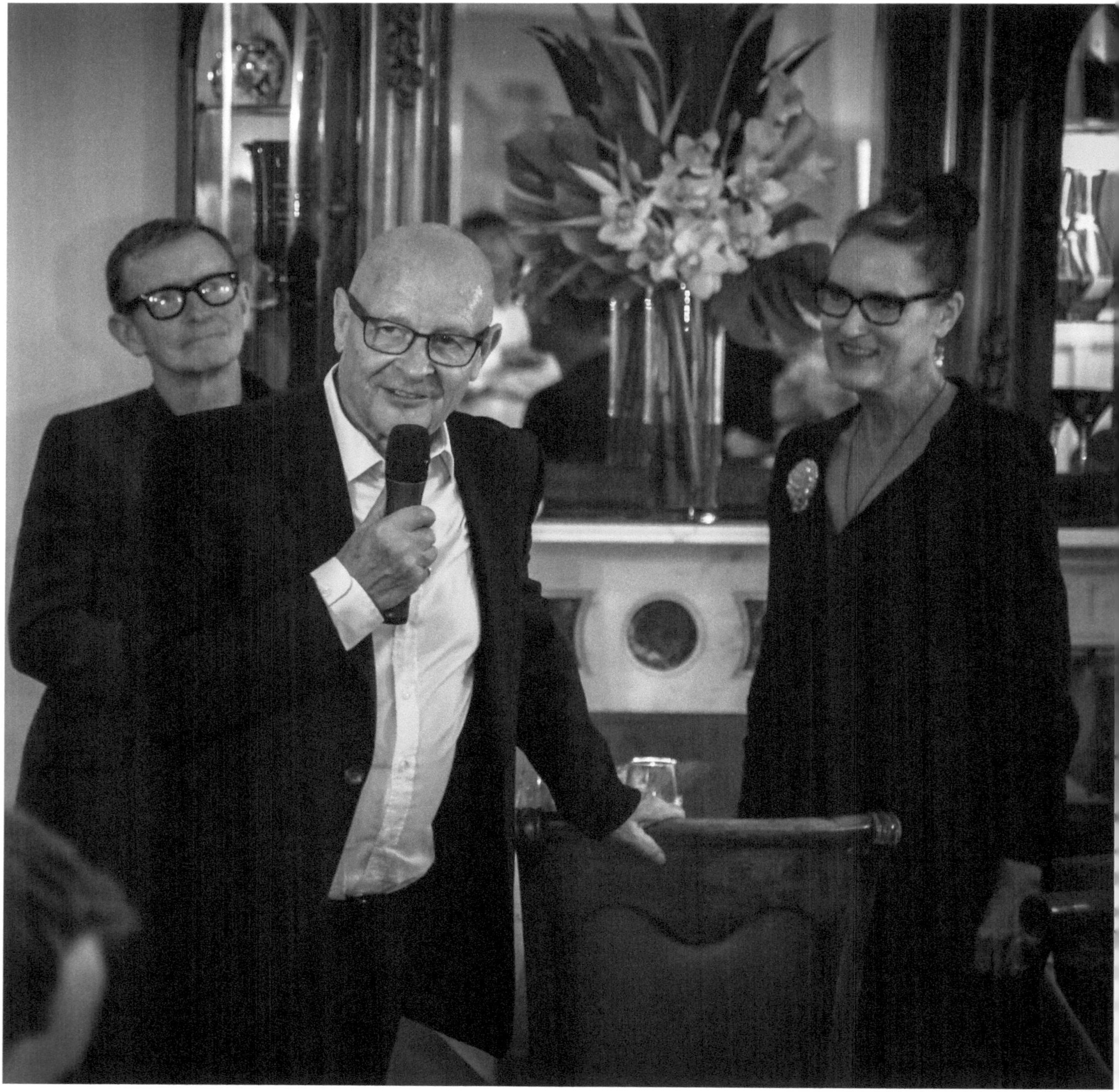

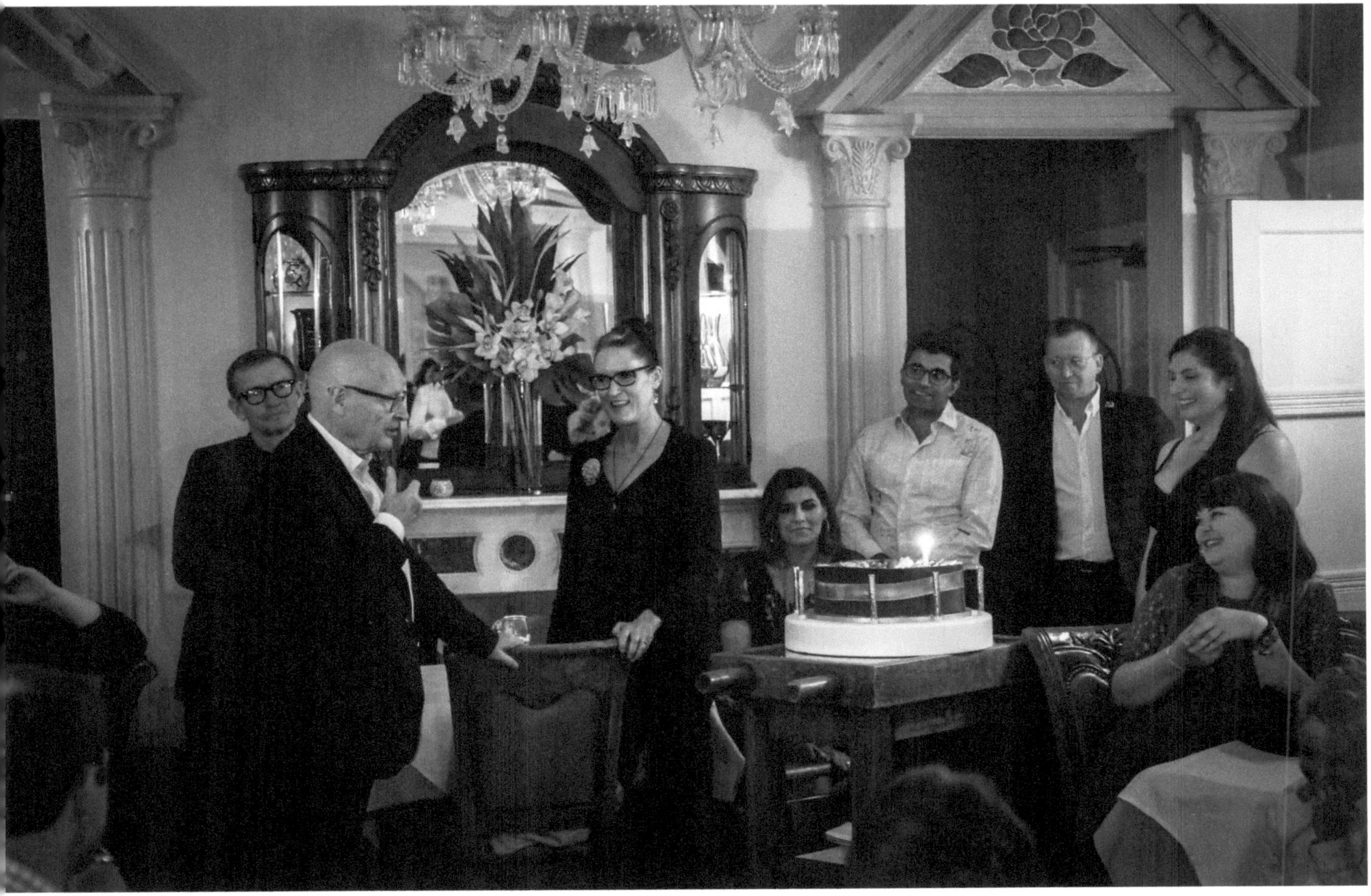

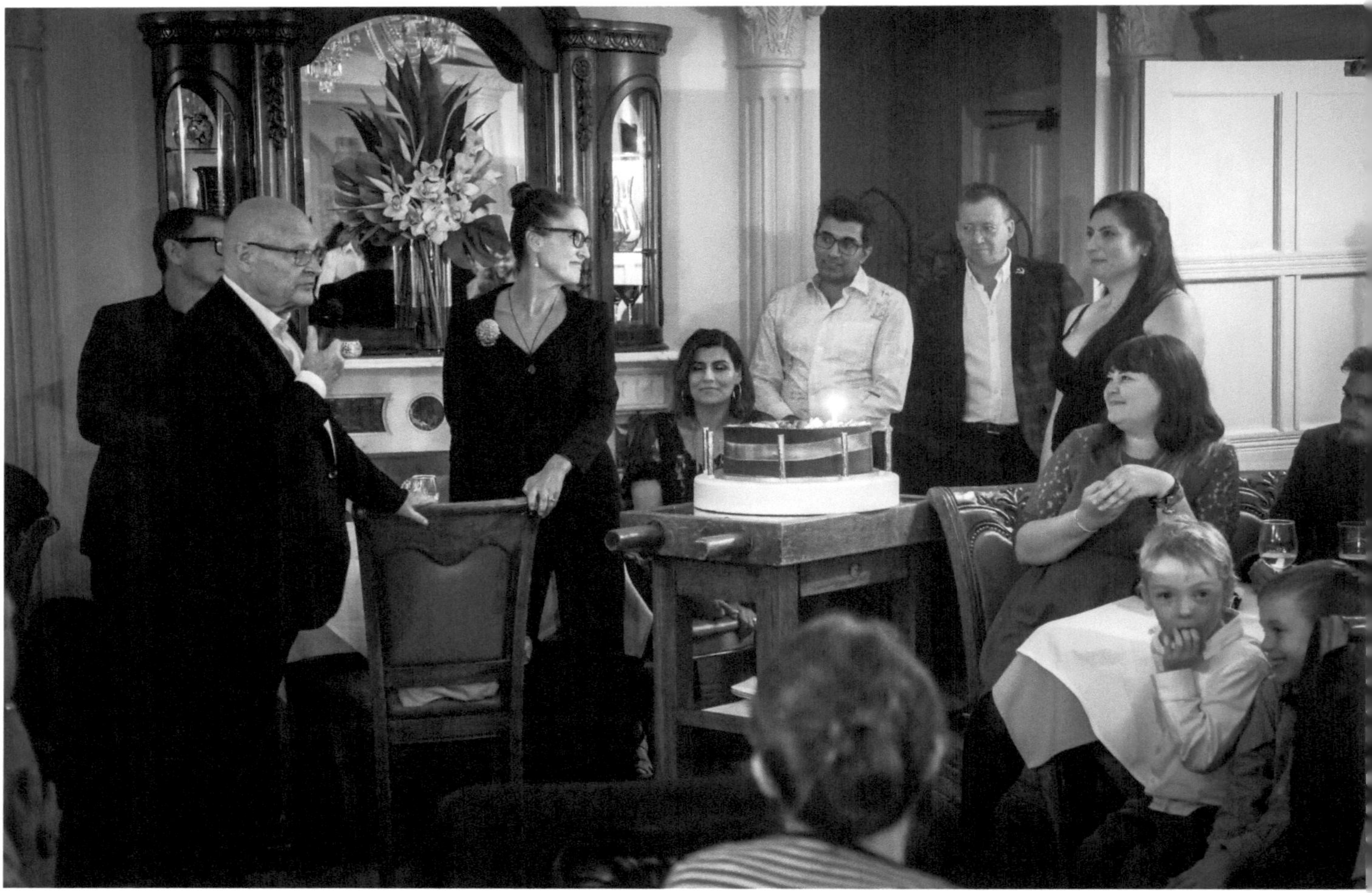

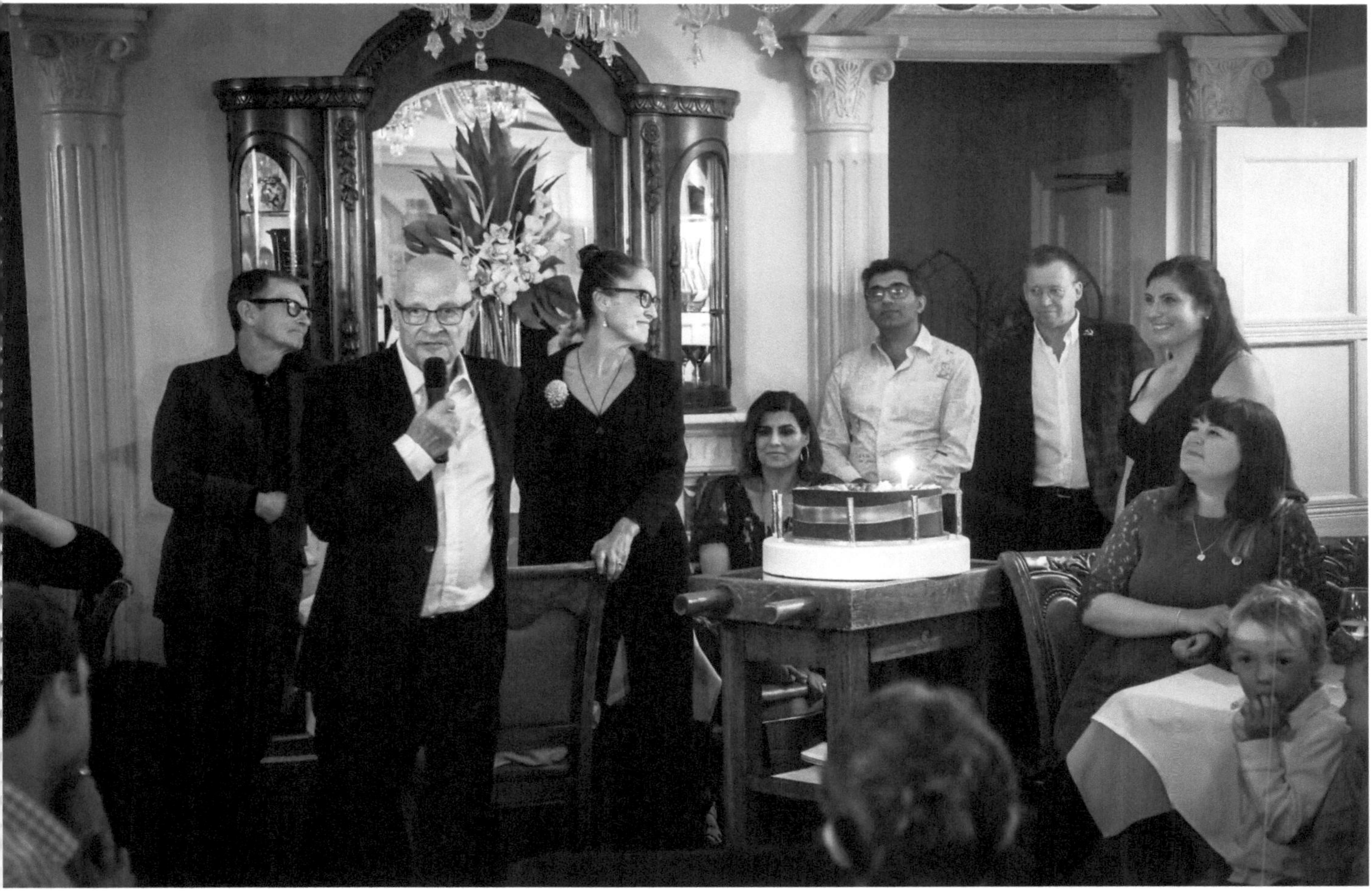

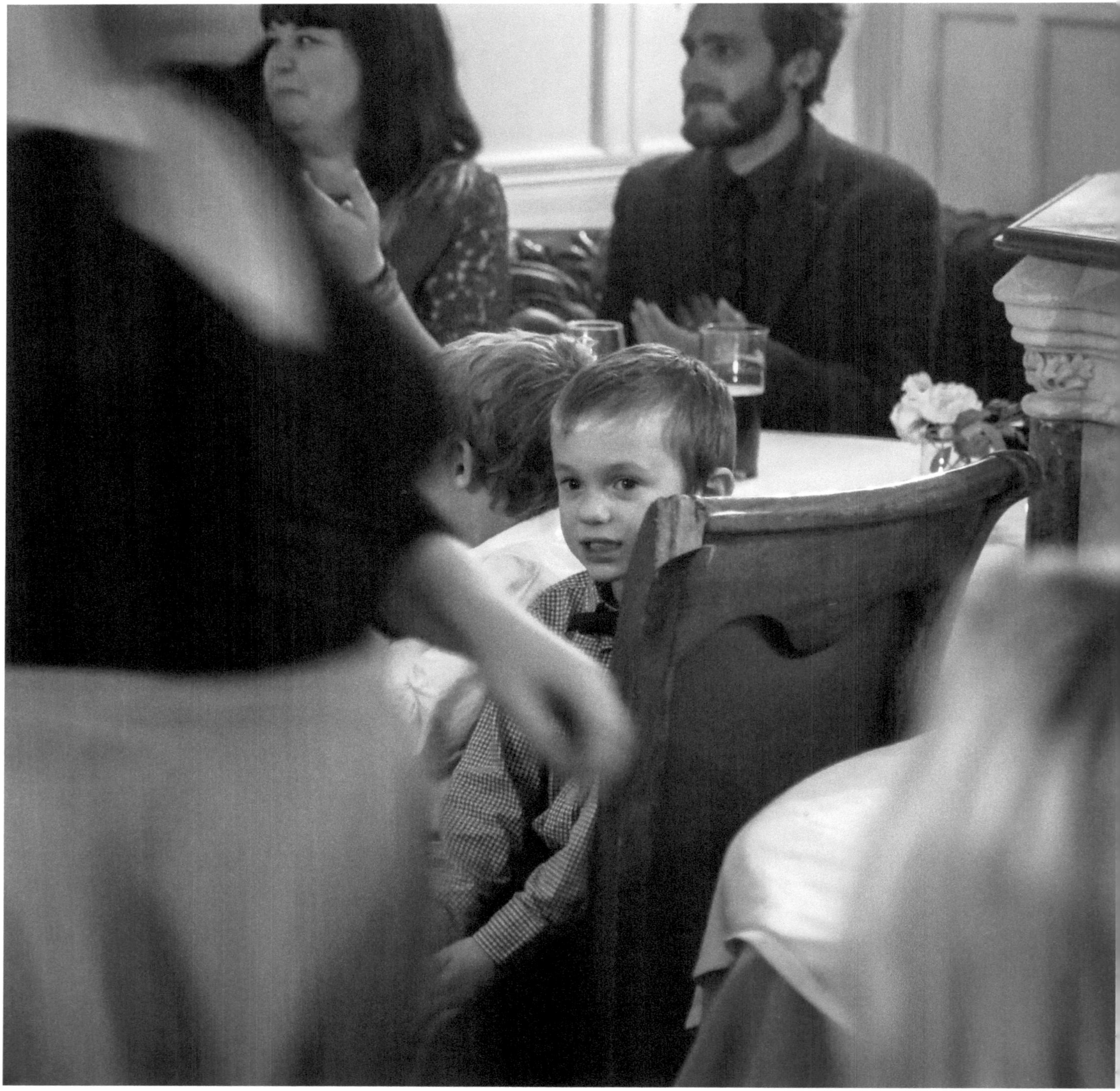

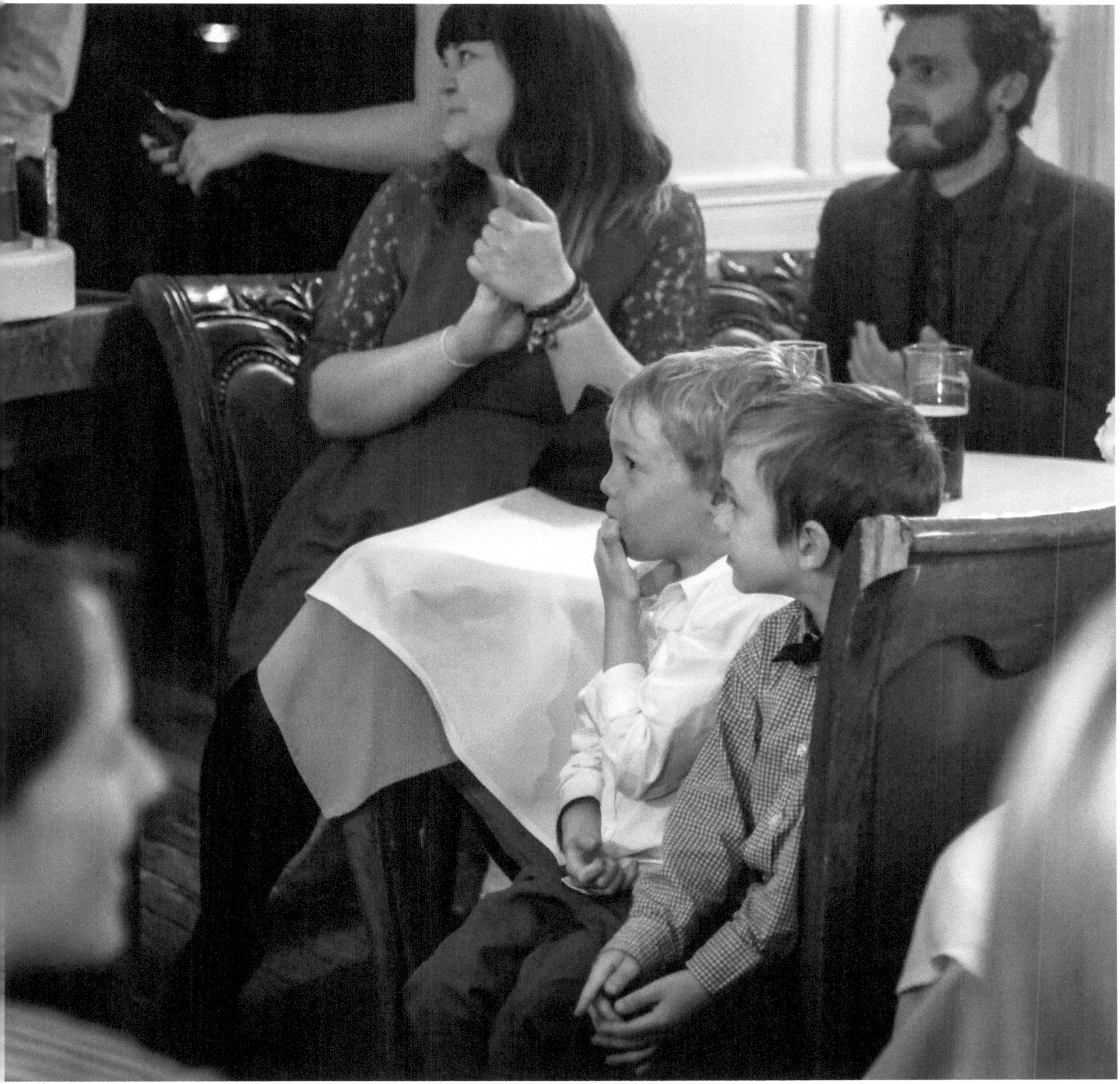

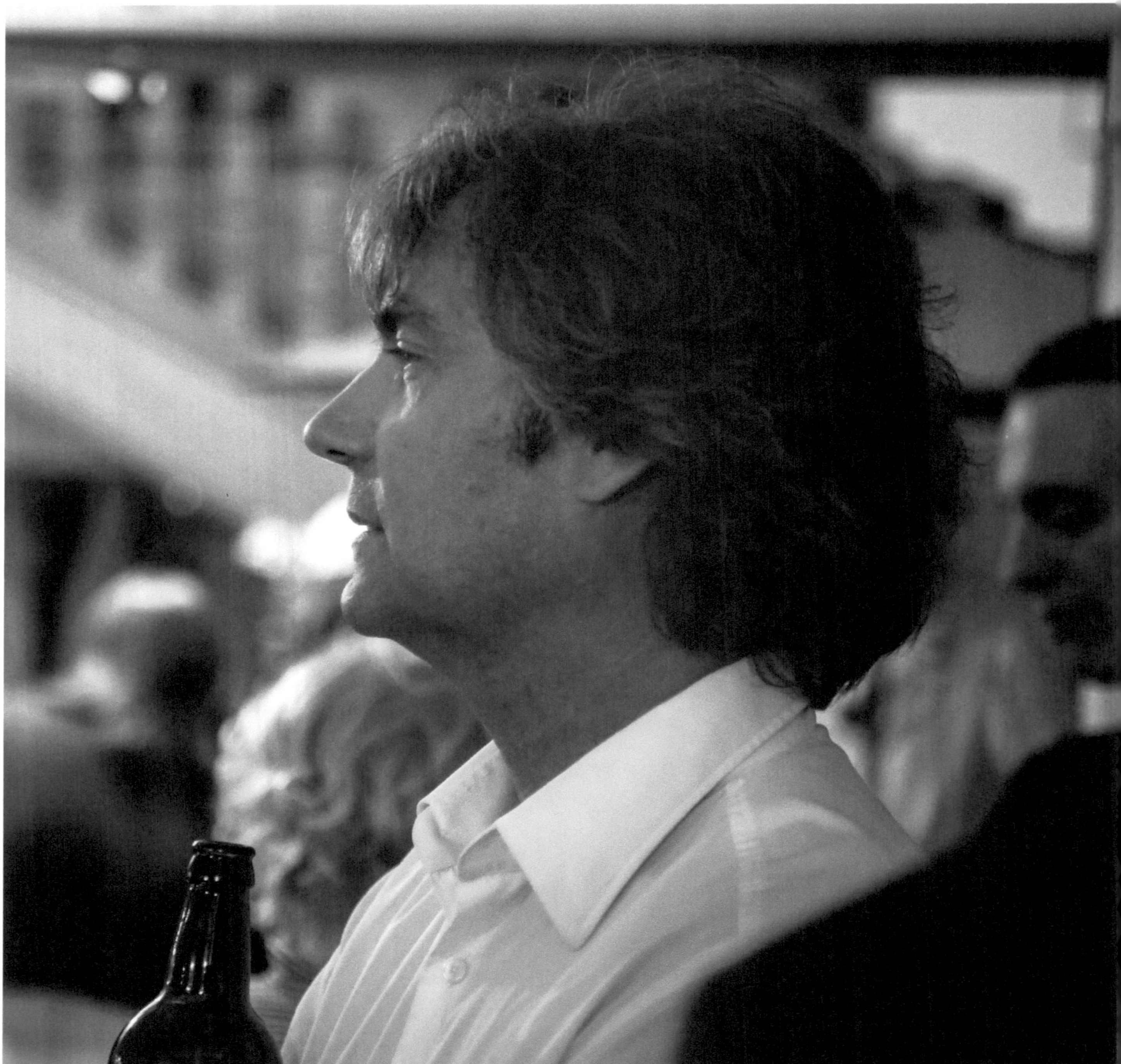

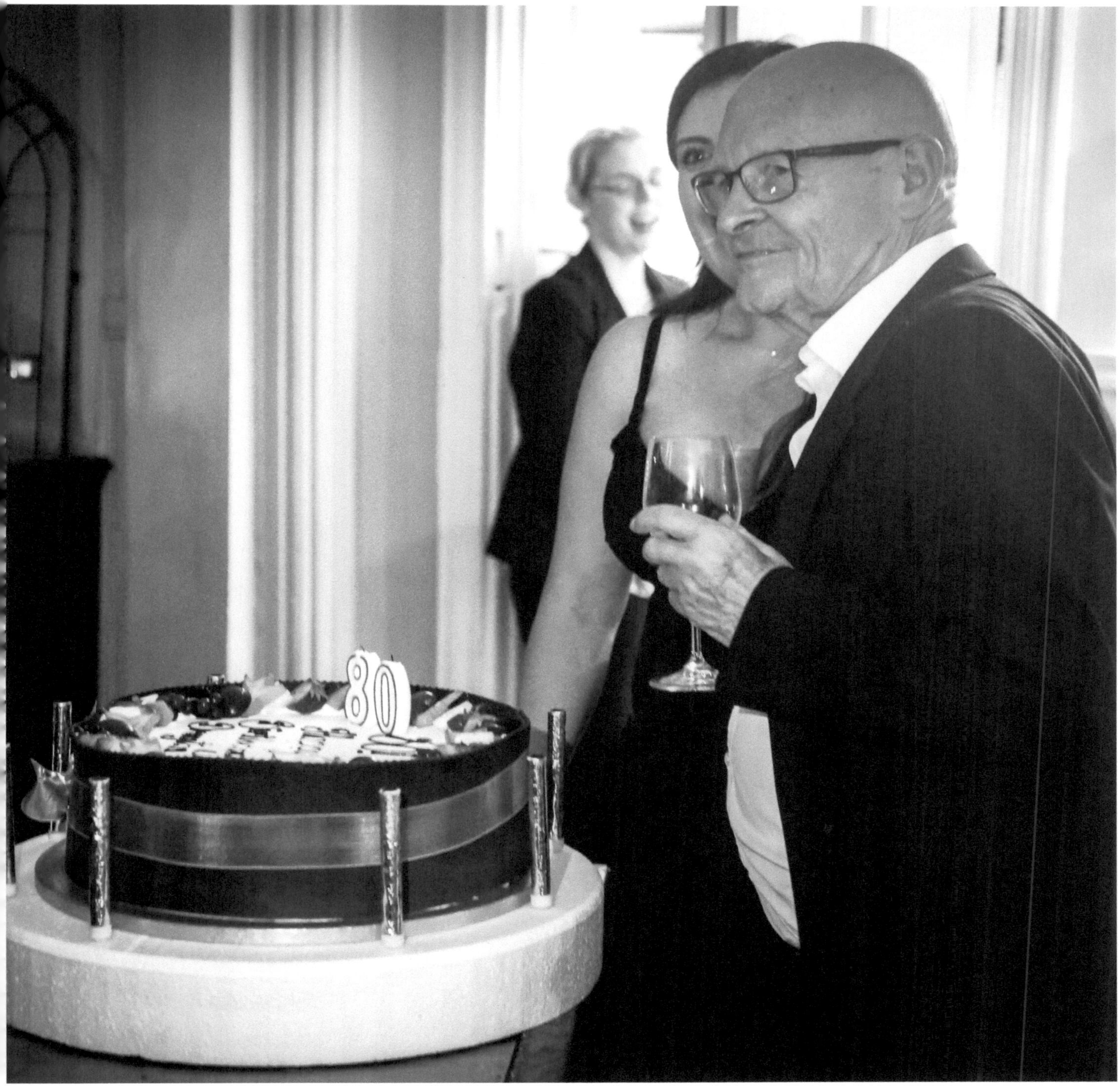
80

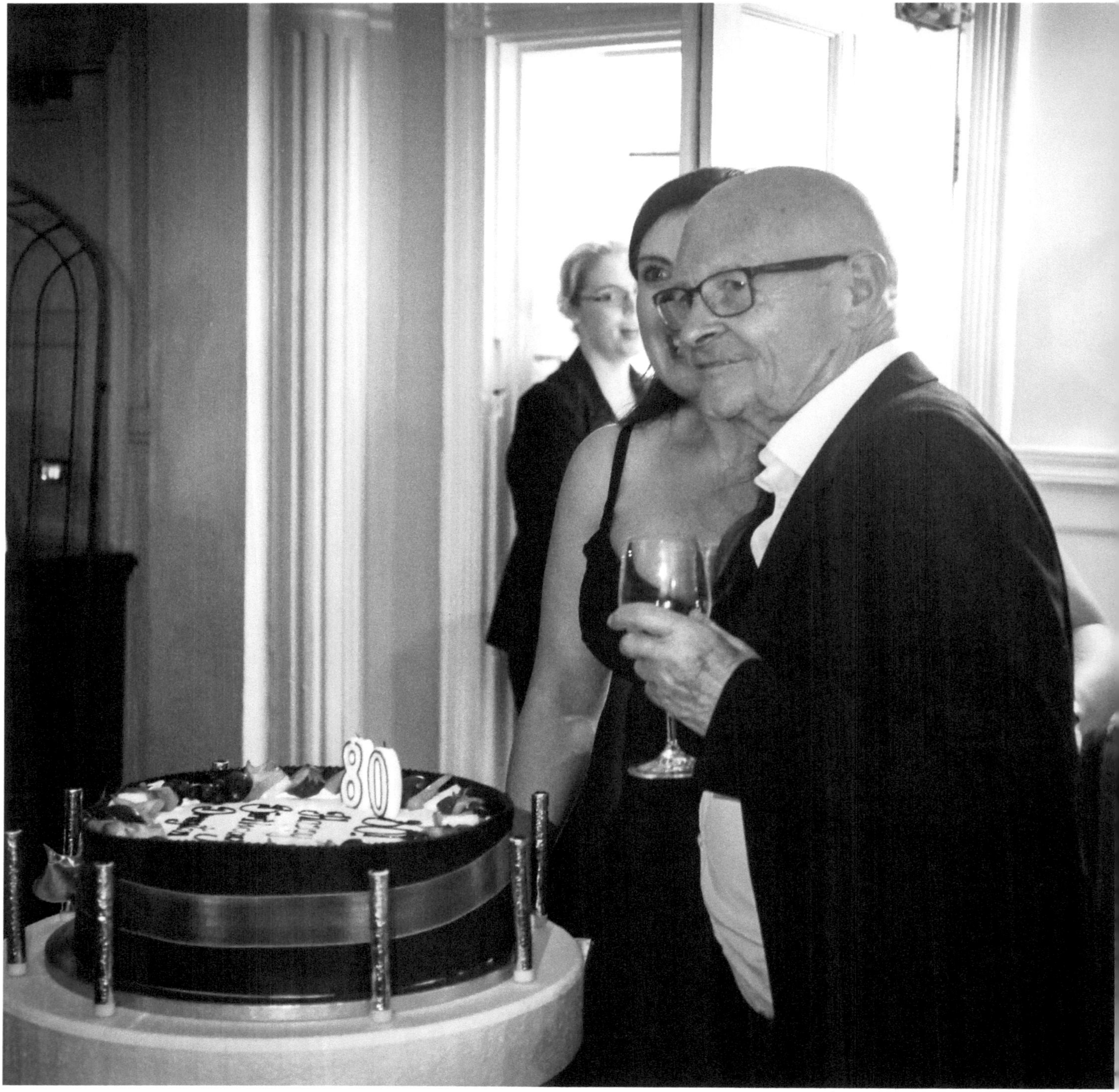
80

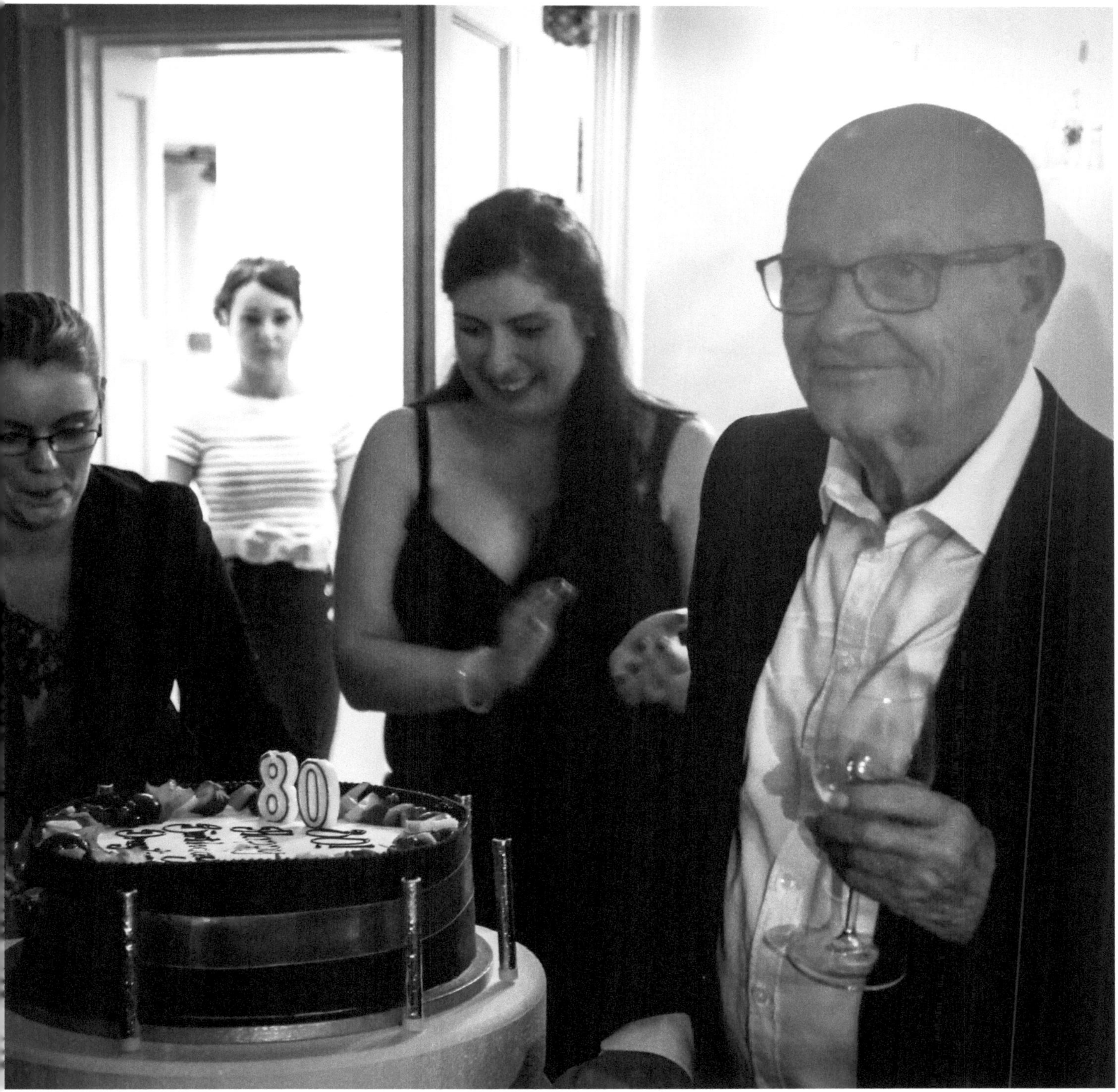
80

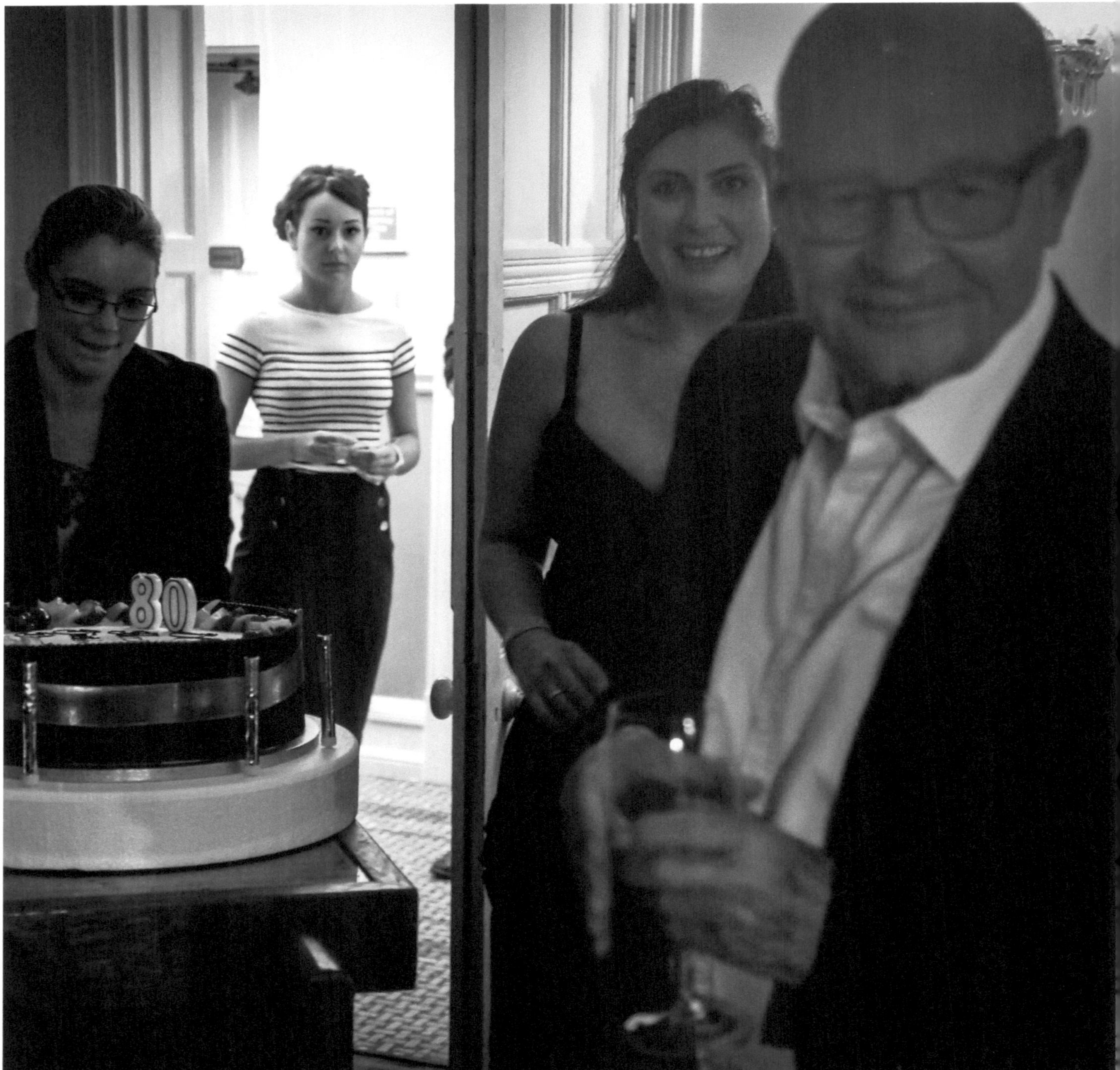
80

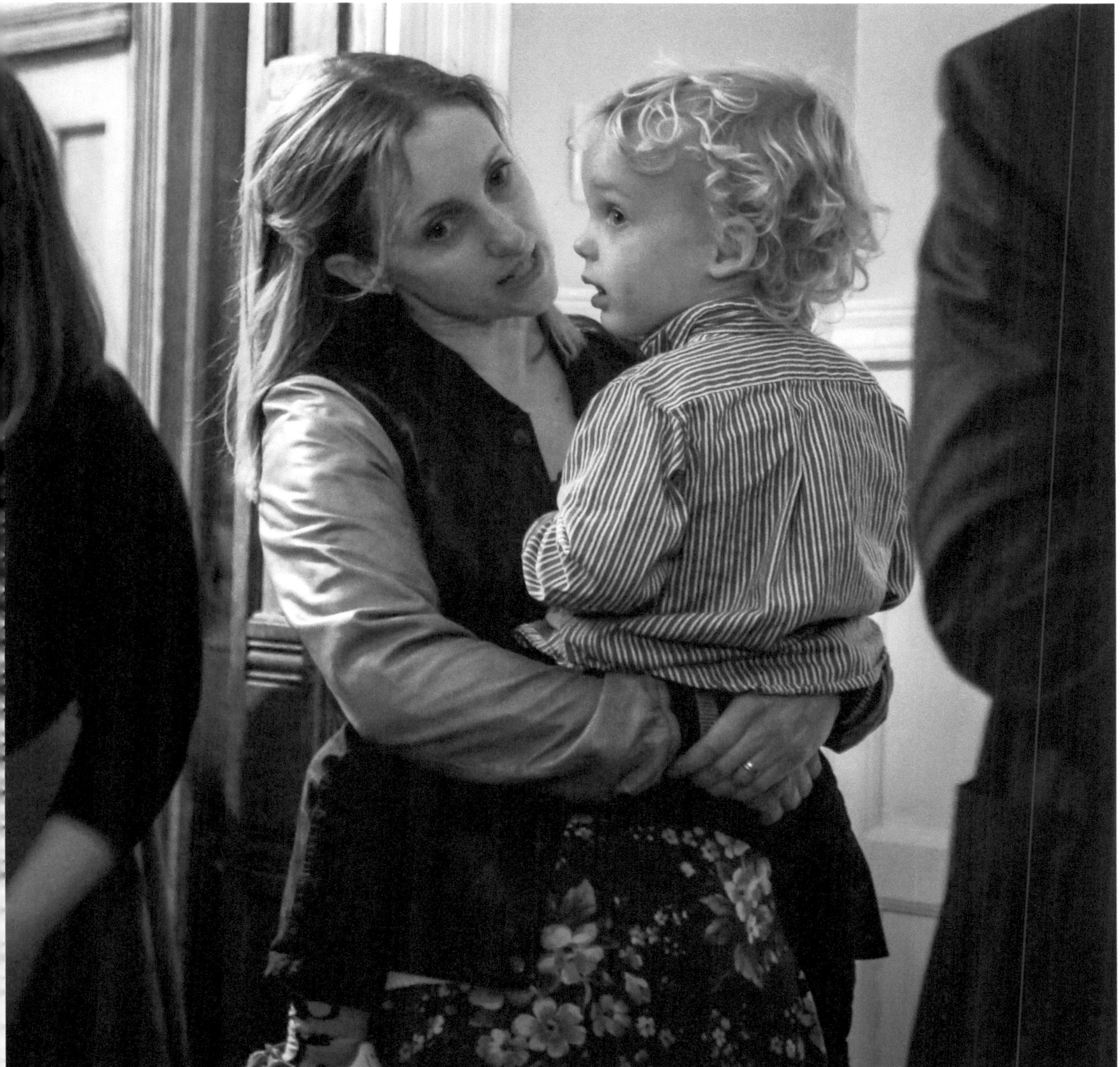

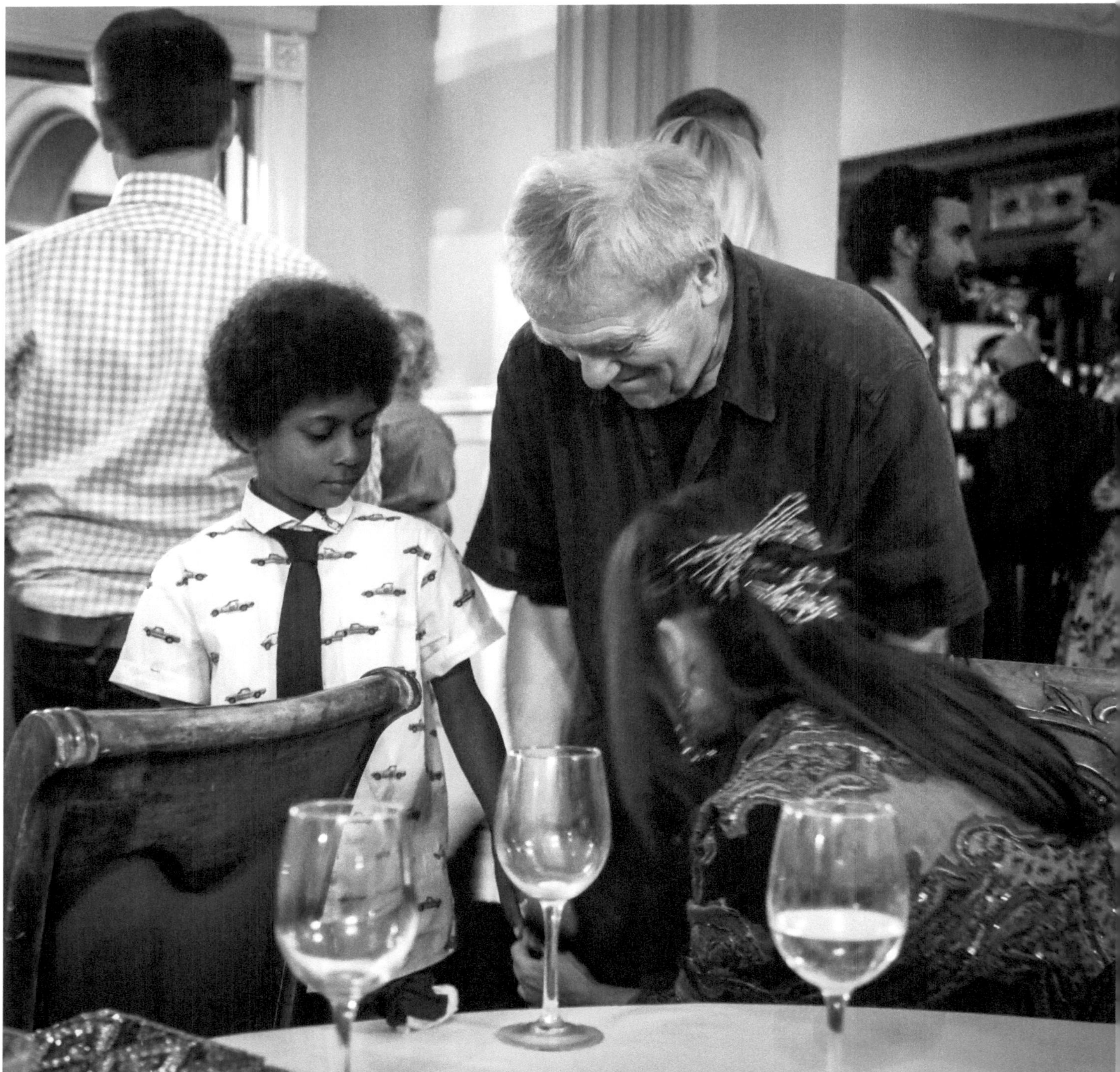

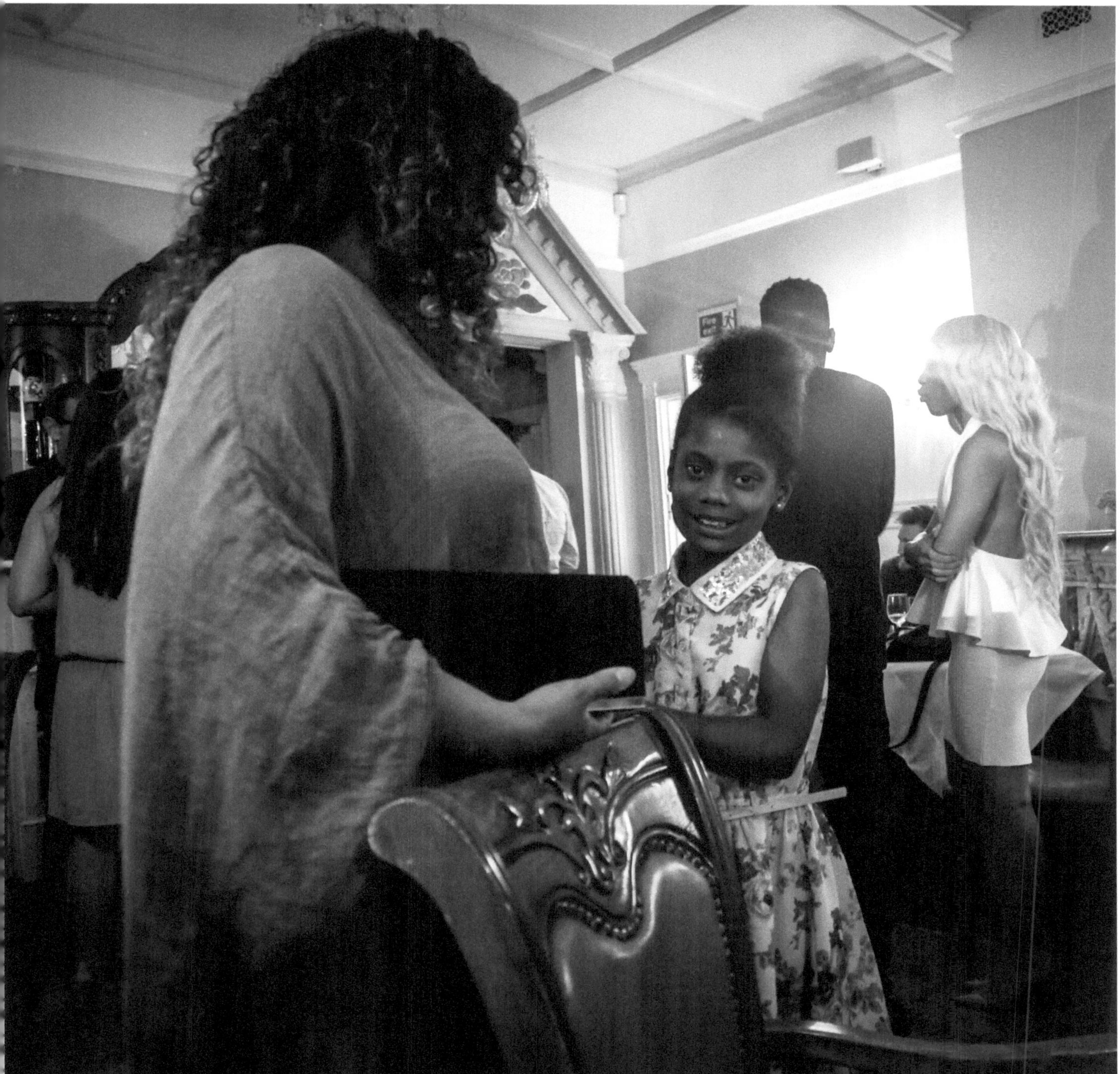

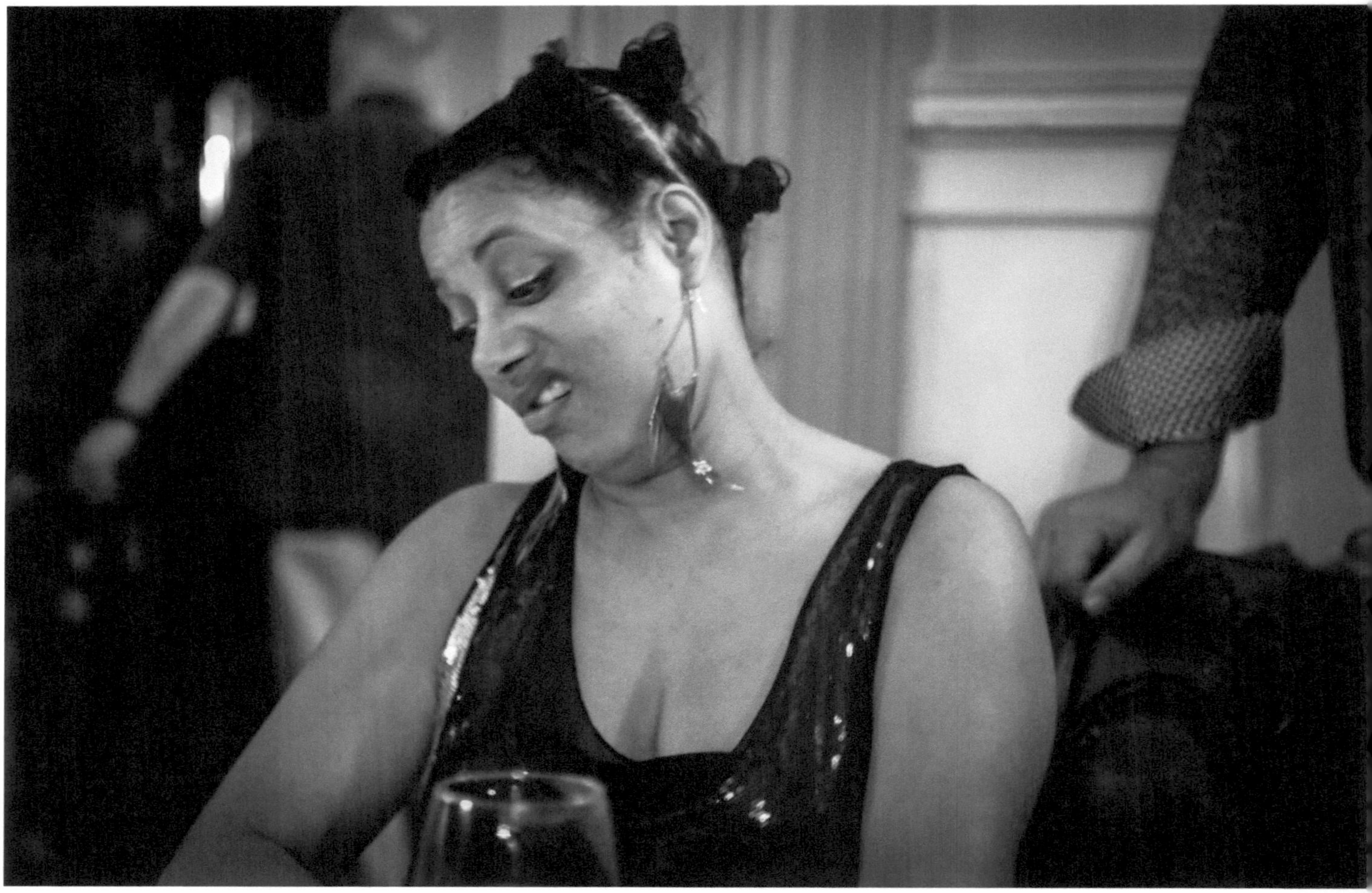

Stop Me and Buy One!

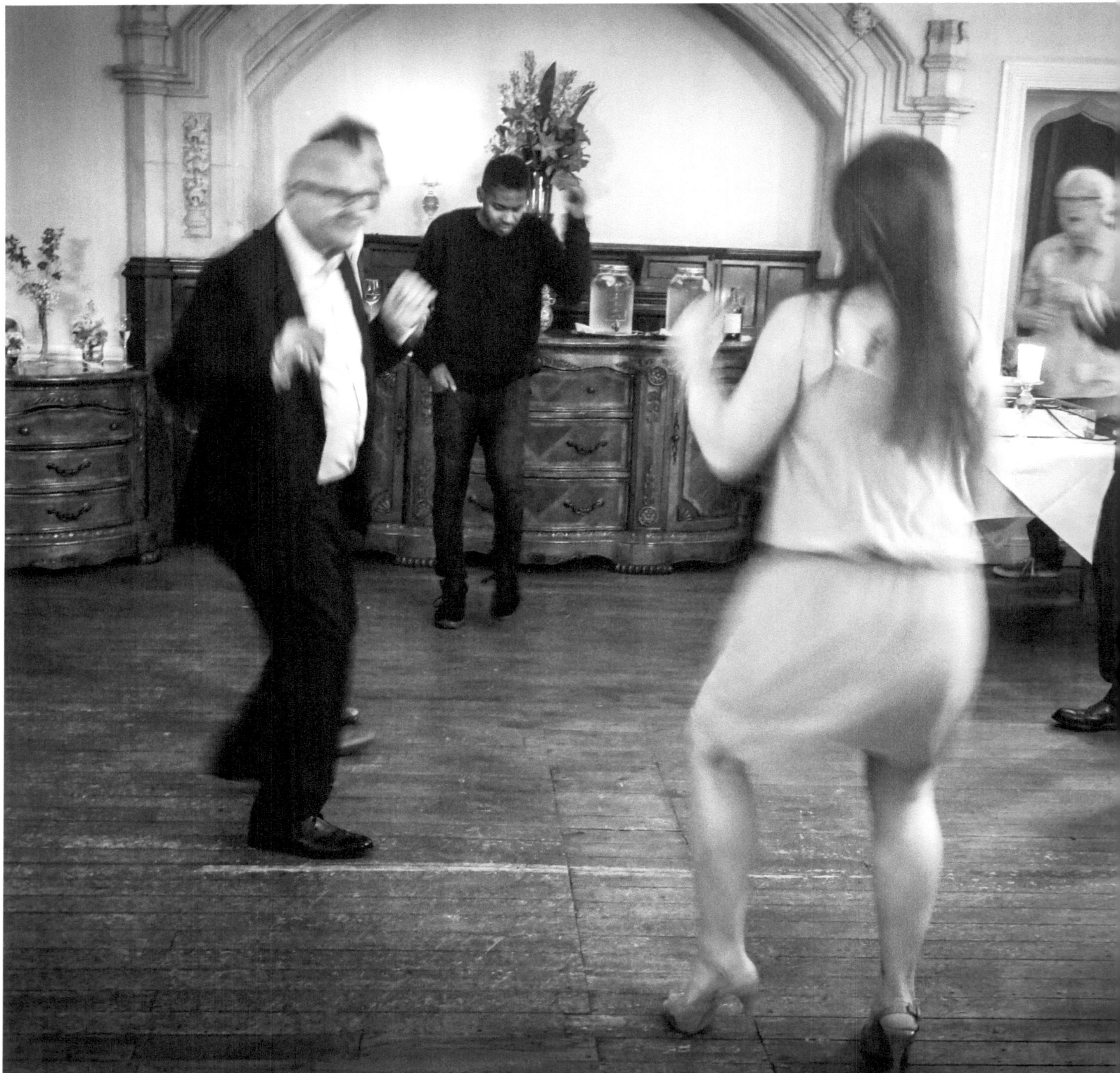

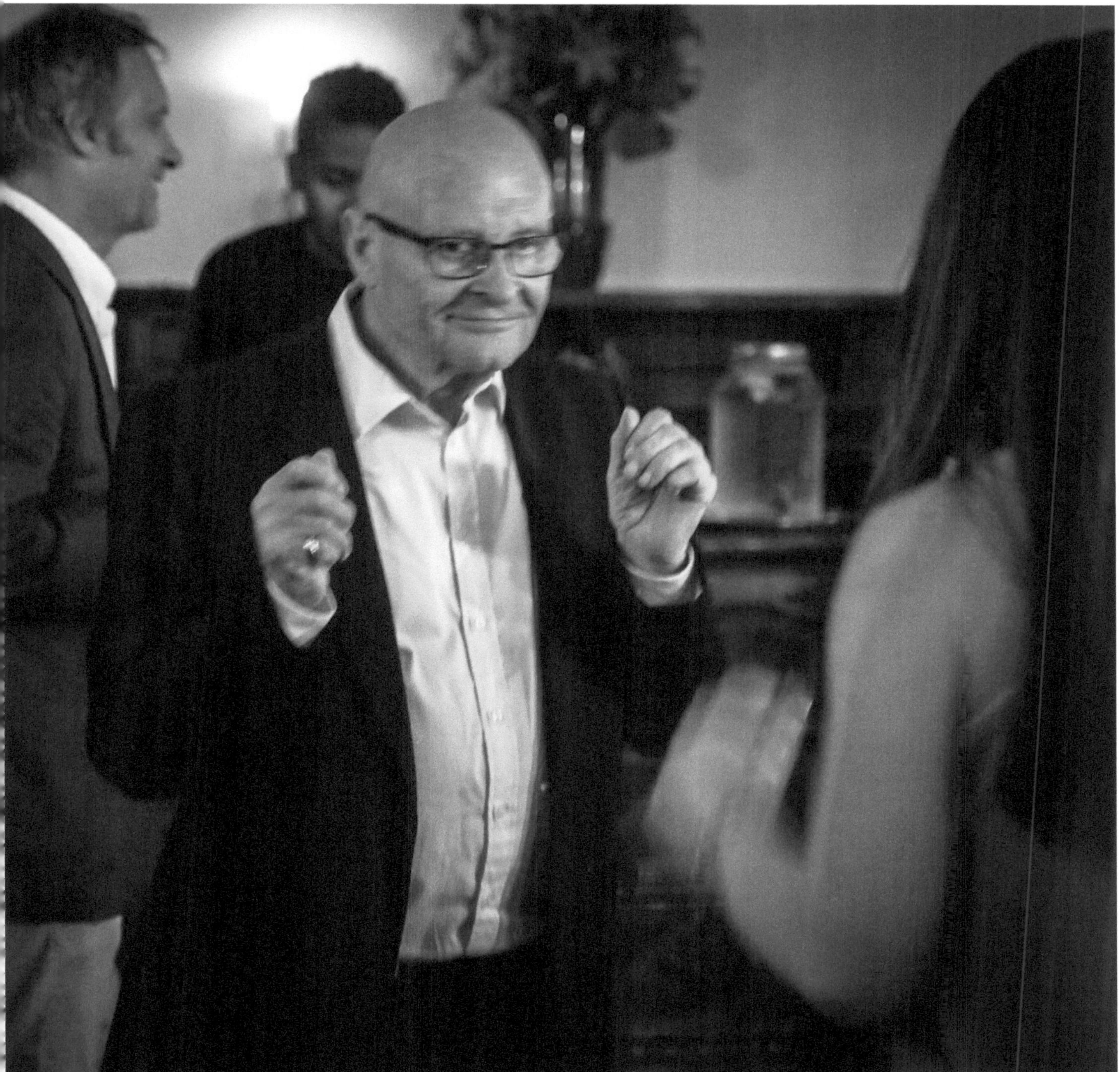

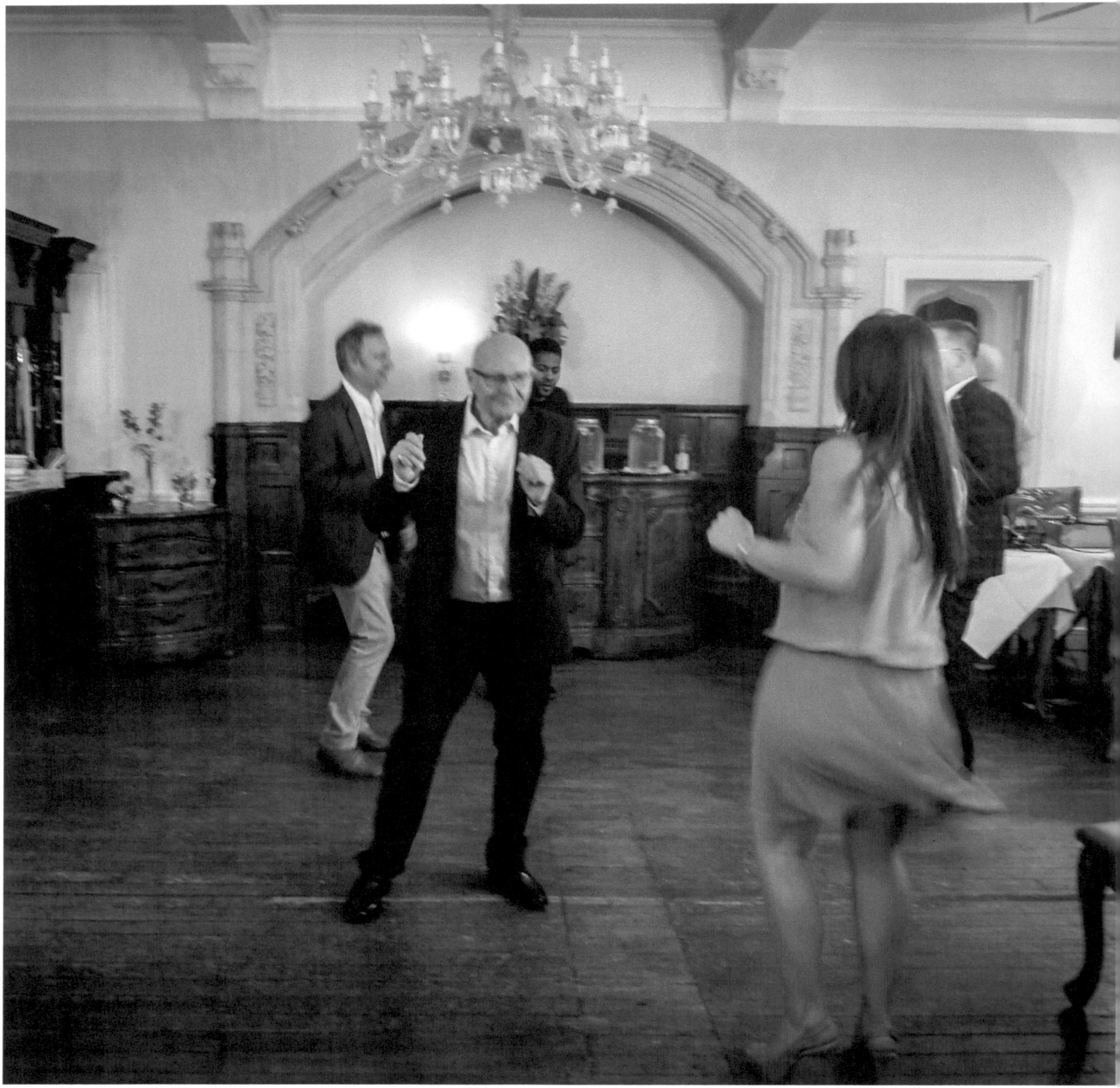

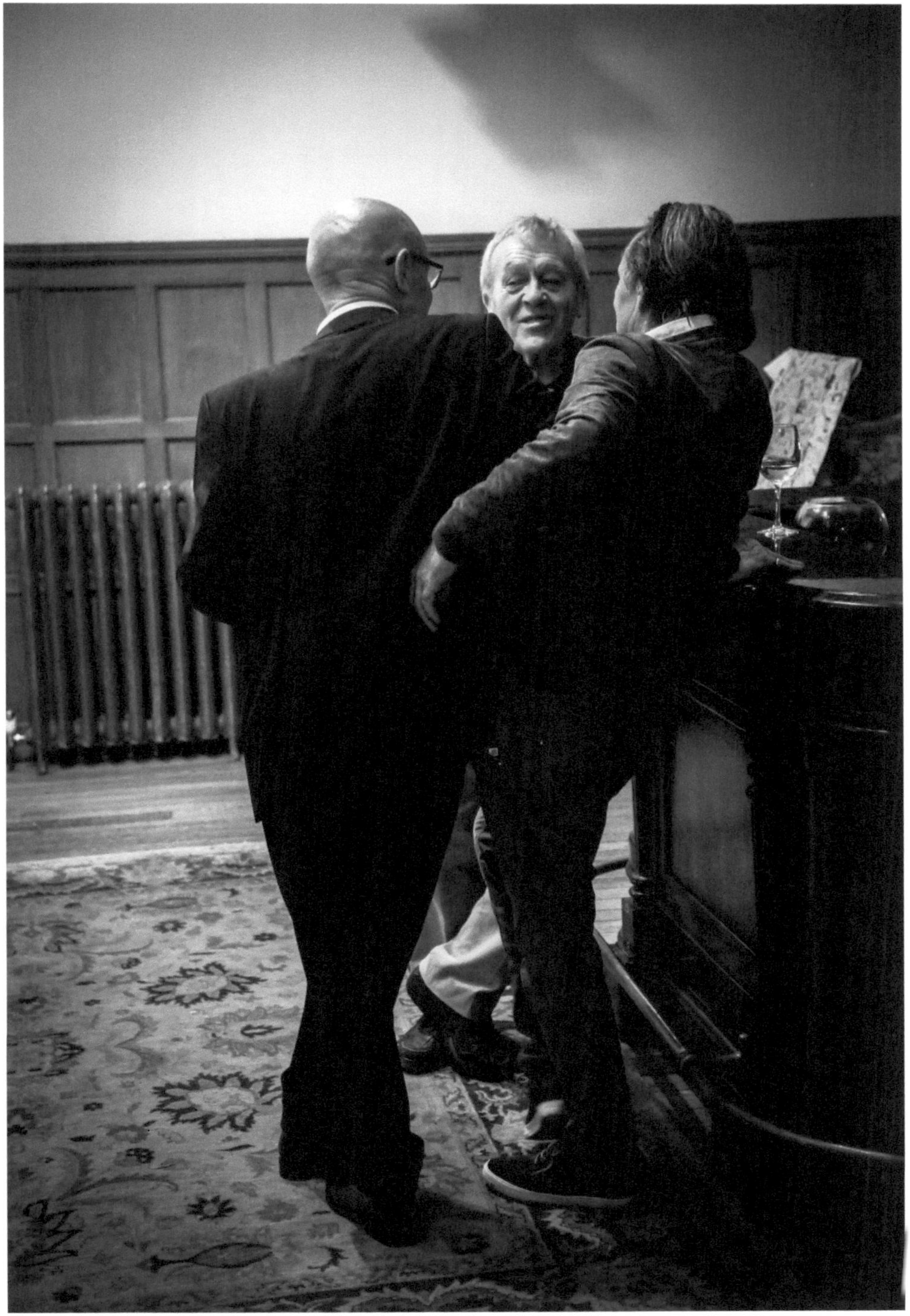

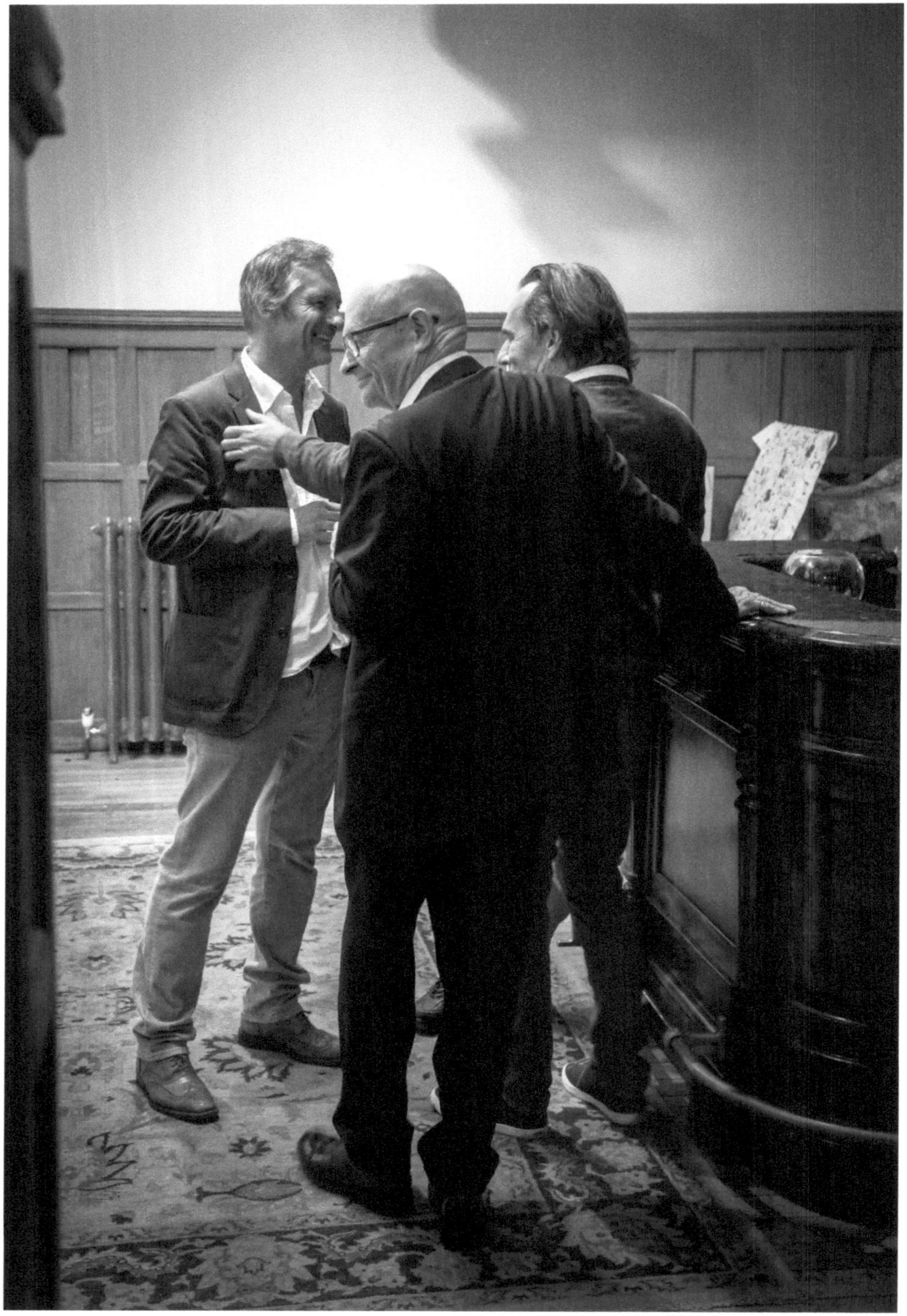

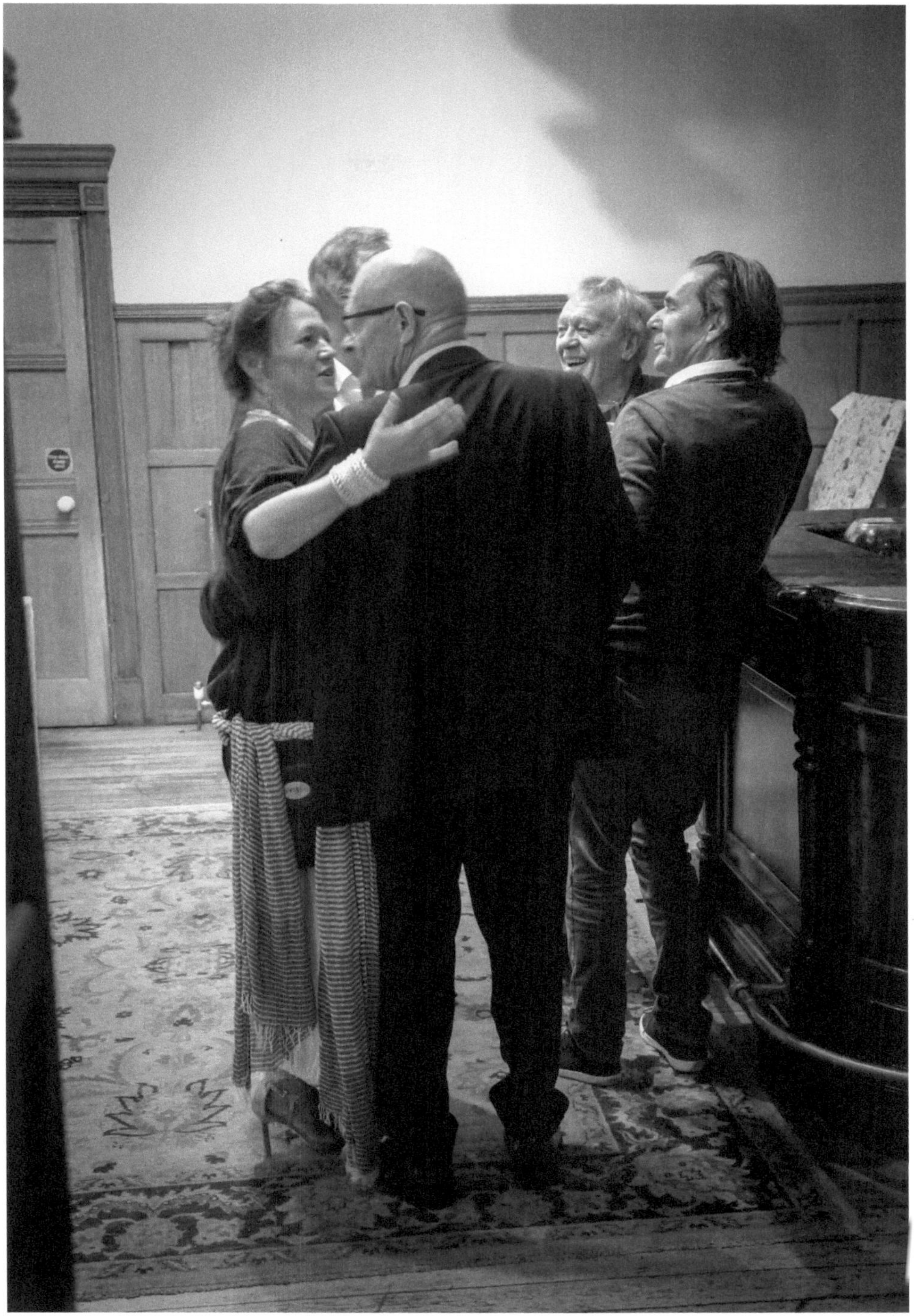

∞0

www.ingramcontent.com/pod-product-compliance
Lightning Source LLC
Chambersburg PA
CBHW040757240426
43673CB00014B/369
* 9 7 8 1 9 9 9 8 8 1 8 9 4 *